TinkerActive WORKBOOKS

2ND GRADE · ENGLISH LANGUAGE ARTS · AGES 7–8

by Megan Hewes Butler

illustrated by Chad Thomas

educational consulting by Lindsay Frevert

Odd Dot · New York

Vowel Sounds

A **fictional text** is a text that describes imaginary events and people. Read this fiction story aloud.

Troubles with Bubbles

Enid and Frank were heading home from school when the bus driver made a wrong turn—and drove the bus into the car wash! Brushes started spinning. Tubes were dripping soap all over the place. A hose shot water to wash it all off. Then ZAP! FIZZ! SLOSH! What was that? Had something broken?

Enid looked out the back window—a giant wave of bubbles was coming! In front of them, a truck had stopped moving. They were stuck!

Enid got an idea. She asked the driver to put the bus in reverse and drive backward out of the car wash. The bus pushed through the water and into the sunlight. Water was gushing out of the car wash, and bubbles came floating into the street. What a mess!

Long vowels sound like their names. For example:

chain

tree

boat

tube

bike

Say each word aloud. Then circle each word with a long vowel sound.

rock

crab

bee

cube

dime

flute

coat

rope

cape

kit

jet

slide

clay

plug

Short vowels sound unlike their names. Write the missing short vowel in each word. Then say each word aloud.

br____ck

m____p

w____b

fr____g

f____sh

fl____g

b____ll

dr____m

cl____ck

br____sh

Read the story on page 2 again. Then write four words from the story that have only short vowel sounds.

_____   _____

_____   _____

Some two-syllable words have both a short vowel *and* a long vowel. Read each word. Then draw a line to connect each word to the correct picture.

Say your name aloud. Does it have short vowel or long vowel sounds? Or both?

Draw a line through the maze to plug in the new bubble maker. Follow a path of only **short vowel** sounds.

CAR WASH

END

fizz

sway

race

wall

grate

snore

honk

slosh

ding

pop

zap

clunk

croak

bam

START

roar

Draw a line through the maze to connect the new hose. Follow a path of only **long vowel** sounds.

LET'S START! GATHER THESE TOOLS AND MATERIALS.

Washable paint

Dish soap

3 small bowls

Spoon

10 drinking straws

Paper

Baking sheet or tray

Light corn syrup

Rubber band

LET'S TINKER!

Say the name of each of your materials aloud. Which ones have short vowel sounds? Which ones have long vowel sounds? **Sort** them into piles by the vowel sounds that you hear.

LET'S MAKE: BUBBLE VOWELS!

1. Place about 1 teaspoon of paint, 2 teaspoons of water, and 4 drops of dish soap into a bowl.

2. Mix them with a straw.

3. Then **blow** carefully to make bubbles! (Repeat steps 1 through 3 with a new color of paint in a new bowl if you'd like more than one color of bubble paint.)

4. Put a piece of paper inside a baking sheet or tray, to contain any drips.

5. Spoon some bubbles onto your paper.

6. Use a straw to blow the bubbles around and make the shape of each vowel.

LET'S ENGINEER!

It's Tinker Town's BIG bubble-blowing contest! Enid is the current champion, and she must defend her belt. This year, Tinker Town has changed the rules—now you can blow bubbles using more than just one object.

How can Enid blow LOTS of bubbles at one time?

Mix 2 tablespoons of dish soap, 5 tablespoons of water, and 1 teaspoon of light corn syrup in a bowl. **Start** by blowing bubbles with one straw, and then add more. What happens? How can your other materials help? How many bubbles can you blow at once?

PROJECT 1: DONE!
Get your sticker!

Nouns & Pronouns

A **poem** is a type of writing that expresses an emotion or idea and sometimes rhymes.

Read the poem aloud.

If I Could Fly

Look up ahead, I see a bee.
First one, then two—I see three!

Now there are more—four, then five.
Where are they from? Where's the hive?

More bees are here. It's a swarm!
Bees buzzing around just like a storm.

A queen and all her worker bees,
Are making a new hive in the trees.

They are building with wax way up high.
I could see them closer if I could fly!

The poem above uses rhyming words to give the poem rhythm. **Bee** and **three** rhyme. Read the poem again and circle other pairs of words at the end of each line that rhyme.

A **noun** is a person, place, or thing. Look at each picture of a noun from the poem and say the name aloud. Then write each noun on the line.

queen
_____

_____

_____

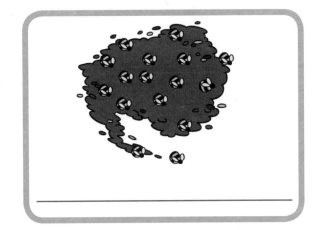

_____

Regular nouns that end in **s**, **sh**, **ch**, **x**, or **z** become plural when you add **es**. Words that end in other letters become plural when you add **s**.

Write each noun again, adding **s** or **es** to make it plural.

_____

_____

_____

_____

_____

_____

Many nouns become plural by adding **s** or **es**. However, some nouns are **irregular** and do not follow these rules.

Read each noun. Then draw a line to match singular and plural forms.

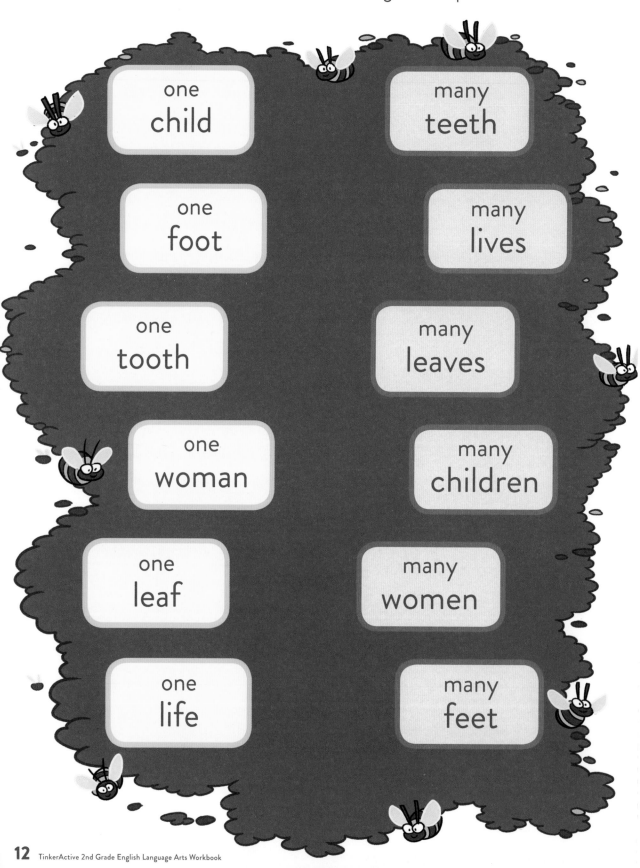

one
child

many
teeth

one
foot

many
lives

one
tooth

many
leaves

one
woman

many
children

one
leaf

many
women

one
life

many
feet

A **collective noun** is a group of people or things.

Draw a line to connect each collective noun to the correct group of people or things.

a herd

a flock

a crew

a class

a deck

a swarm

A **compound word** is when two or more words are joined together to make a new meaning.

Draw a slash between the two nouns that make up each compound word. Think about their meanings. Then circle the picture that matches the compound word.

bird/house

pancake

starfish

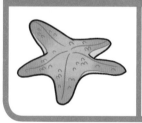 

notebook

Go on a hunt around your home to find these compound words or one of your own. Draw a picture of what you find.

A **pronoun** is a word that takes the place of a noun.

The beehive has honey.

It has honey.

It is a pronoun that can take the place of the noun, **beehive.**

Draw a line from each sentence to the bee or bees the pronoun describes.

He is the biggest.

She has orange stripes.

They are sitting on a flower together.

The ladybug is close to **her.**

The worker bee is flying by **itself.**

The red flower is **his.**

LET'S START! GATHER THESE TOOLS AND MATERIALS.

 Paper

 String

 Toilet paper tube

 Markers

 Paint

 Paintbrush

 Scissors (with an adult's help)

 Drinking straw

 Tape

 Pencil

 2 or more balls (of different sizes)

LET'S TINKER!

Tree rhymes with **bee.** What other words do you know that rhyme with **bee? Use** your materials to make pictures of the rhymes.

LET'S MAKE: FLOWER FOR A BEE!

1. Color a toilet paper tube using markers or paint.

2. Draw two rings around the middle of the toilet paper tube. They should be about the width of your finger apart.

3. Draw straight lines from both rings to the edge. The space between the lines should be about the width of your finger.

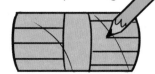

4. Cut each of the lines from the edge to where it touches the ring.

5. Fold each piece of cardboard back to be a petal on the flower.

6. Cut the top 1 inch of a straw in half.

7. Use tape to attach each side of the straw to the flower as a stem.

LET'S ENGINEER!

It's recess time at the Tinker Town school. The MotMots have a ball to play with, and they're not sure what to do with it.

How can they combine "ball" with other activities or objects to have fun?

Write compound words to brainstorm some fun games for the MotMots. **Think** of games you know or make up your own. **Use** your materials to build and play your games.

PROJECT 2: DONE!
Get your sticker!

Read the newspaper article aloud.

TINKER TOWN NEWS

NEW ICE CREAM SHOP IS COOL

Yesterday was an important day for MotMots everywhere. An ice cream shop opened in Tinker Town!

The new store has many flavors: vanilla, chocolate, mint, orange, and even blueberry! There was ice cream in every color. Are you thinking about toppings? There were lots of toppings, too, like sprinkles, cherries, and nuts!

We asked customers in line what they thought of the new store. "It's so COOL!" said one excited little ice cream fan. "I can't wait to come back tomorrow."

Verbs are action words that can tell what happened in the past, present, or future. Rewrite the verb in each sentence in the past tense.

Amelia **rides** to the store.

Amelia ___rode___ to the store.

Enid **sees** the sign!

Enid _____ the sign!

Brian **feels** excited.

Brian _____ excited.

Dimitri **sits** at a table.

Dimitri _____ at a table.

Frank **gives** his order.

Frank _____ his order.

Callie **eats** ice cream.

Callie _____ ice cream.

An **adjective** is a word that describes a noun. Adjectives can describe color, shape, size, and more.

Write an adjective to describe each ice cream order.

Write your own adjective to describe each ice cream order.

An **adverb** is a word that describes a verb, an adjective, or another adverb. Adverbs usually follow a verb in a sentence and often tell when, where, or how something happened.

Circle the adverb that completes the phrase and describes each action.

eating	riding	eating
happily sadly	quickly slowly	carefully messily

banging	standing	sharing
loudly quietly	outside inside	now later

Write your own adverb to describe each action.

eating
_____

talking
_____

tasting
_____

Look at what each MotMot is thinking about. Then write what each one may be thinking. Use the adjectives from the word bank to add details.

cold   fluffy   sweet
giant   chocolaty

_____   _____

_____   _____

_____   _____

_____   _____

_____   _____

Draw the ice cream
you would order! Then
write adjectives to
describe it.

_____

_____

_____

_____

_____

_____

_____

_____

_____

LET'S START! GATHER THESE TOOLS AND MATERIALS.

Small paper bag

Glue

Tape

Scissors
(with an adult's help)

Foam shaving cream

Bowl

Food coloring

Paintbrush

Construction paper

Markers

5 plastic bottle caps

Large handful of pom-poms
(or cotton balls or balls of foil)

LET'S TINKER!

Make a character out of your paper bag and other materials. It can be a model of you, a MotMot, an animal, or even something made up! **Use** your character to act out verbs. Can you make it dance? Sing? Jump? What else can it do? How many verbs can you act out?

LET'S MAKE: ICE CREAM PAINT!

1. Add about 2 tablespoons of glue and ¼ cup of foam shaving cream in a bowl.

2. Choose a color and add 5 drops of food coloring. **Mix** with a paintbrush.

3. On a piece of construction paper, **draw** a cone or a bowl with a marker.

4. Use your paint to add "ice cream"!

5. Let it dry overnight.

6. What adjectives would you use to describe your art?

YUMMY!

LET'S ENGINEER!

There's a heat wave in Tinker Town, and the MotMots are working at The Wobbly Cone. The orders are coming so quickly that they got all mixed up! The MotMots need to match each order with the correct customer.

How can they describe each order to the customers to find the correct match?

Use bottle caps as bowls, roll paper into cones, and use pom-poms as scoops of ice cream. Then **build** five of your own mini orders. **Glue** them together and use your other materials to make and add toppings. Then **write** three adjectives that you could use to describe each order on paper. **Describe** each order's color, shape, size, or taste.

PROJECT 3: DONE!
Get your sticker!

Word Building

A **science fiction** story is made up about a world where science plays a big part. There can be spaceships, time travel, or even creatures from other planets! Read the science fiction story aloud.

ROBOT EMERGENCY

Everything was running smoothly at the robot factory. Robot after robot came down the assembly line. So I didn't think that it was a big deal to go and grab a snack. (All I did was make some popcorn.) But when I returned, instead of a shiny row of metal robots, I saw a mess! It was a robot emergency!

On my right I saw a toothless robot. On my left I saw a headless robot. Robots were rolling out of the machine with missing parts—or parts in the wrong places! A robot stumbled by on a leg and an arm.

How fast could I stop this mess? And how would I ever undo it?

While I was frozen in place, a tall and powerful robot unlocked the control panel. He pressed a red button I had never seen before. POP! The robot machine made a loud noise. Then it started making robots even faster than before! Robots of all different shapes, sizes, and colors were shooting out.

DO NOT
X
TOUCH!

I dropped my popcorn and ran for help as fast as I could. Could the robots ever be stopped? I needed backup!

Read the word that describes each robot. Then use stickers from page 129 to add the missing parts back on the robots.

The suffix **-less** means **without**.
Head**less** means **without a head**.

headless **armless** **legless**

toothless **footless** **noseless**

Prefixes are special sets of letters that can be added to the start of a word to make a new word. Knowing what a prefix means can help you figure out unknown words. Read the two prefixes below.

re- means **again**

un- means **do the opposite of**

Combine each prefix with the word next to it and write the new word. Then draw a line to match each new word with a robot.

un+wind _unwind_

re+paint _____

re+build _____

un+lock_____

re+fill _____

un+tie _____

Suffixes are special sets of letters that can be added to the end of a word to make a new word. Knowing what a suffix means can help you figure out unknown words. Read the two suffixes below.

| -ful means **full of** | -less means **without** |

Combine each suffix with the word next to it and write the new word. Then draw a line to match each new word with a robot.

color+ful _____

name+less _____

cheer+ful _____

tooth+less _____

power+ful _____

A **root word** is a word without any prefixes or suffixes.
Underline each root word.

button / re<u>button</u> / un<u>button</u> / <u>button</u>less

repaint

toothless

unzip

powerful

undo

unbuild

colorful

joyful

relock

retie

footless

joyless

Read each word. Then draw a robot to match the description.

headless

joyful

unhappy

helpful

LET'S START!

GATHER THESE TOOLS AND MATERIALS.

Cardboard tubes, small boxes, and small plastic leftover containers

Old magazines

Scissors
(with an adult's help)

Glue

Paper

Foil

Tape

LET'S TINKER!

The prefix **un-** means **do the opposite of; reverse**. **Use** your materials to explore: What can you stack and unstack? What can you roll and unroll? What else can you do and undo?

Look around your home—can you find anything to lock and unlock, tie and untie, or button and unbutton?

LET'S MAKE: COLLAGE ROBOT!

1. Cut out 20 pictures of things from a magazine.

2. Choose one to be your robot body and glue it in the middle of a piece of paper.

3. **Think** about the other parts your robot should have: a head, arms, hands, and fingers? How many legs will your robot have? What about a light, a claw, antennae, or buttons? **Choose** a picture for each part and glue it on the paper.

LET'S ENGINEER!

Tinker Town's fire department wants to start using a robot to find fires and put them out. But they're not sure what the robot should look like or what parts it would need.

How can the MotMots build a robot that would be good at finding and putting out fires?

Design and build your own firefighting robot. What parts will your robot need? A hose for arms? A siren for the mouth? **Take** cardboard tubes, small boxes, or plastic containers and cover them in foil. **Use** tape to hold the foil in place. Then **glue** the parts together to build the body. **Tape** or glue on other materials to add more details. Will your robot be colorful? Powerful? Cheerful? **Describe** it!

PROJECT 4: DONE!
Get your sticker!

Free verse poems have no patterns or rules. They don't even have to rhyme.

Read the poem aloud.

Up, Up, Up!

I'm growing up, up, up.
I was in first grade,
And now I'm in second.
If you'd like to listen, I've learned a lot.
I can do a cartwheel.
Rolling.
   Spinning.
      Jumping.
And I can pack my own lunch.
Cleaning.
   Cutting.
      Counting.
I can even tie my shoes,
All by myself.
What will I be able to do next?
I'm growing up, up, up!

The poem "Up, Up, Up!" uses repeated lines and alliteration to give the poem rhythm.

A **repeated line** is when a phrase or line of the poem is used more than one time.

Write the repeated line from the poem on the previous page.

_____

_____

Alliteration is when the same beginning letter or sound is used in two or more words that are close together.

Read these phrases aloud. Underline the words that have alliteration.

If you'd like to listen, I've learned a lot.

And I can pack my own lunch.
Cleaning.
Cutting.
Counting.

Read the poem aloud.

I can do a cartwheel.
Rolling.
   Spinning.
     Jumping.

Draw a picture of Callie acting out each word.

ROLLING	**SPINNING**	**JUMPING**

Read each set of words and act them out. Then follow the directions.

walk   **stomp**   **march**   Circle the action that is the **loudest**.

look   **peek**   **stare**   Circle the action that takes the **longest**.

touch   **tap**   **bang**   Circle the action that is the **softest**.

Read the poem aloud.

> *And I can pack my own lunch.*
> *Cleaning.*
>   *Cutting.*
>   *Counting.*

Look at each picture closely. Draw a line connecting each word to the matching picture.

cleaning   cutting   counting

Write about and draw other actions that you can do to help make snacks or meals.

_____

_____

Write your own thoughts and feelings about growing up.

I am _____ years old.

I am in _____ grade.

What are you **proud** that you can do?

_____

_____

_____

_____

_____

_____

What makes you feel **happy** about growing up?

_____

_____

_____

_____

_____

_____

_____

_____

What do you hope you can do when you get older?

_____

_____

_____

_____

_____

Write your own free verse poem about getting older. This poem doesn't have to use any patterns or rhymes to share your thoughts and feelings. Include information you wrote on the previous page.

Try using repeated lines and alliteration in your poem.

Share your poem with a friend or family member!

LET'S START!

GATHER THESE TOOLS AND MATERIALS.

Crayons

Cardboard

Scissors
(with an adult's help)

Paper cup

20 or more pennies

20 drinking straws

String

Tape

LET'S TINKER!

Arrange your materials by size, and then **describe** the size of each object: Which ones are small, tiny, or itty-bitty? Are any big, huge, or gigantic? What other sizes of materials do you have? What other ways can you sort your materials by size?

LET'S MAKE: ALL ABOUT ME!

1. **Use** a crayon to draw the first letter of your name large on a piece of cardboard.

2. With the help of an adult, **cut** it out.

3. Think of 5 words that start with the same letter as your name. They can be words that describe you or names of things that you like. **Write** these alliteration words on your letter.

4. Use crayons and stickers from page 129 to decorate your letter.

LET'S ENGINEER!

The Tinker Town airport is rebuilding their control tower, and they want to add a helipad so helicopters can land right on top of the building!

How can the MotMots design a tower that can hold the weight of a helicopter?

Use a paper cup with 20 pennies inside to act as your "helicopter." **Design** and build a tower using your materials that can hold the empty cup. Then **add** pennies one at a time—how many pennies can you add before the tower falls? How can you change your design so that it is bigger and stronger?

PROJECT 5: DONE!
Get your sticker!

Working with Unknown Words

Callie's dog, Boxer, started training school last week. Read Boxer's diary and the dictionary definitions aloud.

DATE: APRIL 1

Today is my first day at school. I don't know anyone! I feel very **nervous**. Will I like my teacher? Who will I play with at recess? Will I meet any new friends? I am also feeling very **timid**. I am too shy to make new doggy friends.

DATE: APRIL 2

I made it through my second day at training school! Today I decided to be **brave**. I said "Woof!" to a dog named Bella. She was so nice! We played together at recess. I am feeling **optimistic.** I have hope that I can meet more new doggy friends tomorrow.

DATE: APRIL 3

Today was my third day at school, and it was great. I played with Bella at recess again. I said "Woof!" to more dogs, and I made new doggy friends! I am feeling **relieved.** I am calm and relaxed because I don't feel alone at school.

relieved
adjective – \ ri-ˈlēvd\
experiencing or showing relaxation, especially from anxiety or pent-up emotions

brave
adjective – \ˈbrāv\
having or showing courage and boldness

optimistic
adjective –
\ˌäp-tə-ˈmi-stik\
feeling hopeful about the future

nervous
adjective – \ˈnər-vəs\
anxious, apprehensive

timid
adjective – \ˈti-məd\
showing a lack of courage or self-confidence

Read each word that describes how Boxer felt. Then draw a line to connect the word to a matching picture.

brave

nervous

optimistic

relieved

timid

Act out the meanings of these five feeling words!

Read each sentence aloud, and look at each underlined word. Circle the word below each sentence that means the same thing.

At school we have to eat fast because lunchtime is **brief**.

short   long

I had **chunky** muffins with pieces of fruit inside.

smooth   lumpy

I wanted to be **gutsy**, so I said "Woof!" to more new dogs.

shy   brave

They tasted so **superb** that I ate all five!

awful   great

They were so **puny** that five fit in my paw.

tiny   large

Bella couldn't eat her whole muffin because it was too **massive**.

big   small

A **homograph** is a word that is spelled like another word but that is different in meaning.

Read each sentence. Then circle the picture that shows the correct meaning of the homograph.

Callie's name starts with the **letter** C.

Boxer is writing a **letter** to the teacher.

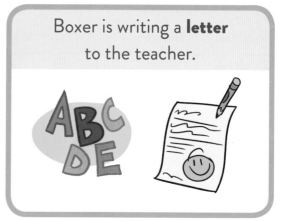

Callie learned to **tie** a knot.

Boxer wore a costume with a fancy **tie**.

Callie put the class pet back in the **pen**.

Boxer got a new **pen** for writing.

The word **duck** is also a homograph. Write a sentence for each meaning.

_____

_____

Write and draw your own diary page. Use a dictionary to help you spell any unknown words.

DATE: _____

_____

_____

_____

_____

_____

_____

_____

You can use feeling words from Boxer's diary. Check the spelling in the dictionary definitions on page 42.

LET'S START! GATHER THESE TOOLS AND MATERIALS.

Book

Dictionary
or online dictionary

Paper
or notebook

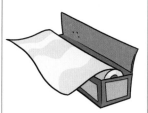
Wax paper

Markers

Yarn or string

Scissors
(with an adult's help)

School glue

Bowl

Ink pad

LET'S TINKER!

Open up a book and find the first word that you don't know. **Look** it up in a dictionary or online dictionary. Then **use** your materials to make a picture of it.

LET'S MAKE: LOOPY LETTERS!

1. Tear off a piece of wax paper about the size of a notebook.

2. Write the first letter of your name on the paper. **Write** it large and take up the whole page.

3. Cut about 20 pieces of yarn, each about the length of your hand.

4. Squeeze some glue into a bowl.

5. Dip each piece of yarn in the glue, one at a time. **Place** the yarn on the letter.

6. Let the letter dry and then peel it off the wax paper.

The word "letter" has more than one meaning. You've made a letter from your name. Can you use your materials to make another kind of letter?

LET'S ENGINEER!

Boxer keeps mixing up Callie's feelings. When she's sad, he thinks it's time to play. When she's happy, he sits in a corner by himself!

How can Callie show Boxer different feelings?

Make five faces that show different feelings. **Press** your thumb into an ink pad and then onto a piece of paper. Then **use** a marker to draw features that make a face: like eyes, a nose, and a mouth. **Write** a feeling word that describes each face. You can **use** a word that you know or a new one that you learned in this project. You can also **look up** a new one in a dictionary or online dictionary.

PROJECT 6: DONE!
Get your sticker!

A **fable** is a short made-up story that often uses talking animals to teach a lesson. There is usually a hero and a villain in the story. Read the fable aloud.

The Lion and the Mouse

One day a mouse was playing in the bright, leafy woods. He raced down tall trees and jumped over logs. He was running so fast that he ran right into the nose of a sleeping lion! The lion woke up and caught the tiny mouse with his giant paw. The mouse shook with fear! "Please let me go! If you help me, someday I will help you," he begged. The lion let out a huge roaring laugh. Someone so tiny could never help him! He got such a good laugh that he decided to be kind and let the mouse go.

Later, the lion was roaming the woods. He was looking for his next snack when SWOOSH! He accidentally stepped into a trap hidden by a hunter. A net lifted him off the ground—he was stuck. "HELP!" he roared at the top of his lungs.

The mouse heard the roaring from far away and ran through the branches as fast as he could. When he got to the lion, he jumped up and started chewing the net. In a few minutes he chewed through the rope and set the lion free! "You laughed at me," the mouse reminded the lion. "You said that a mouse could never help a lion. But now you know! You can't judge what someone can do by how they look. Even someone tiny can be a giant hero."

Read the fable again. Try using different voices for the characters.

Write a ✔ next to why the mouse ran into the lion.

- ☐ He was running too fast.
- ☐ He wanted to meet the lion.
- ☐ He had stepped in a trap.

Circle how the mouse felt when the lion caught him.

Write a word you would use to describe this feeling:

_____

Circle how the lion felt when the mouse promised he would help the lion.

Write a word you would use to describe this feeling:

_____

Write a ✔ next to what the lion did to the mouse.

- ☐ He kept the mouse.
- ☐ He let the mouse go.
- ☐ He asked the mouse to help him someday.

Write a ✔ next to why the lion stepped into a trap.

- ☐ The trap was made of rope.
- ☐ The trap was gone.
- ☐ The trap was hidden.

Write and draw to answer these questions about the story.

WHO were the characters?

_____   _____

HOW did the characters meet?

_____

_____

WHERE was the setting? Add details from the story to your drawing.

_____

WHEN did the lion need help?

_____

_____

WHY do you think the mouse helped the lion?

_____

_____

_____

_____

WHAT do you think would have happened if the mouse had not chewed through the lion's rope? Draw what might have happened below. Then tell a friend or family member the new ending to the story.

Write the numbers 1, 2, 3, and 4 to put the illustrations in order from first to last.

In a fable, there is often a lesson, called a **moral**.

What moral did the lion learn about how he treated the mouse?

_____

_____

_____

_____

What moral did YOU learn?

_____

_____

_____

_____

Draw a picture of a time that a friend helped you.

Draw a picture of a time that you helped a friend.

Label yourself and your friends
in the drawings.

LET'S START!

GATHER THESE TOOLS AND MATERIALS.

Small toy

String

Plastic bottle

Scissors
(with an adult's help)

Cardboard

Glue

Shoebox

Construction paper

Paint

LET'S TINKER!

In the fable, the mouse helped the lion escape from a net. **Find** a toy that you can wrap in string, like the lion in the net. How can you free the toy? Could any of your other materials help?

LET'S MAKE: LIVELY LION!

1. With the help of an adult, **cut** the bottom off a plastic bottle and recycle the top half.

2. Cut a flower shape and tail shape, each about as long as your hand, out of a piece of cardboard.

3. Paint the pieces to be the lion's body, head, and tail.

5. Glue the head on the front of the bottle, and the tail on the back.

4. Add a sticker from page 129 to the flower shape for the lion's face.

LET'S ENGINEER!

Callie is setting up a Fable Table at Tinker Town's art fair. She is going to tell her own fables! She made a few animals, but she doesn't have any settings where she can tell her stories.

How can Callie make settings for her Fable Table?

Make or build your own setting to tell a fable or story. **Decide** where your story will take place—at school, the park, a store, the beach, or someplace else. Then **use** your materials to decorate the inside of your shoebox to look like that setting.

PROJECT 7: DONE!
Get your sticker!

Reading Informational Texts

Read this informational text aloud.

The History of Skyscrapers

Skyscrapers are very tall buildings, including the tallest buildings in the world! Skyscrapers have changed a lot over time. As builders and engineers use new designs and materials, the buildings they make keep getting taller.

In 1857 an inventor took an important step toward building the very first skyscrapers. Elisha Otis designed an elevator that was safe for people to use every day. Before this, people had to use the stairs! Now it made sense to build taller buildings because people could go up and down easily.

The first skyscraper was built in Chicago in 1885—over one hundred years ago. It was only ten stories tall! The city was growing fast, and people needed buildings that were taller but also strong and safe. It was the first building to use a grid made of steel beams, which made it very sturdy.

Many taller skyscrapers continued to be built in the United States, including the Empire State Building and the Sears Tower. Then, in 1998, the tallest building ever built was finished in Malaysia. Ever since then, the tallest skyscrapers have been in other countries around the world.

Using new designs and materials, skyscrapers continue to be built higher and higher. In fact, the meaning of the word "skyscraper" had to change! Most people now say a skyscraper must be over 490 feet tall. That's four times taller than the first skyscraper! However, the current tallest building in the world, the Burj Khalifa, was built in 2010 and is much taller than that: 2,717 feet. But this record won't last for long. New and taller skyscrapers are still being built.

Have you ever seen a skyscraper?

☐ Yes   ☐ No

A **main idea** is the most important thought or point of a passage or paragraph.

Write a ✔ next to the **main idea** of the passage.

☐ **The first skyscraper was 10 stories tall.**

☐ **Skyscrapers have changed a lot over time.**

☐ **A skyscraper must be over 490 feet tall.**

Draw a circle around the paragraph with this main idea:

The elevator was an important invention that led people to build buildings taller.

Put a ✔ next to the event that happened first.

☐ **The first skyscraper was built in Chicago.**

☐ **The tallest skyscraper in the world was built in Malaysia.**

☐ **Elisha Otis designed the first safe elevator.**

Put a ✔ next to the event that happened last.

☐ **The Burj Khalifa was built.**

☐ **The Empire State Building was built.**

☐ **The Sears Tower was built.**

Answer each question about "The History of Skyscrapers."

Who invented the first safe elevator? _____

Why was this invention important?

_____

_____

Where was the first skyscraper built? _____

When was it built? _____

What is the tallest building in the world right now?

_____

How tall is it?

_____

How tall do you think the tallest skyscraper will be in a hundred years?

_____

What do you think it will look like? Draw and write your answer.

Write one question about something that you still want to know about skyscrapers. Use a question word, like **Who**, **What**, **Where**, **When**, **Why**, or **How**, to begin your sentence.

_____

_____

_____

Tell a friend or family member one new fact you learned about skyscrapers!

Informational texts can share information by using pictures, charts, diagrams, and more. A **timeline** is a chart that shows the order in which events occured. It often includes dates to tell when each event happened.

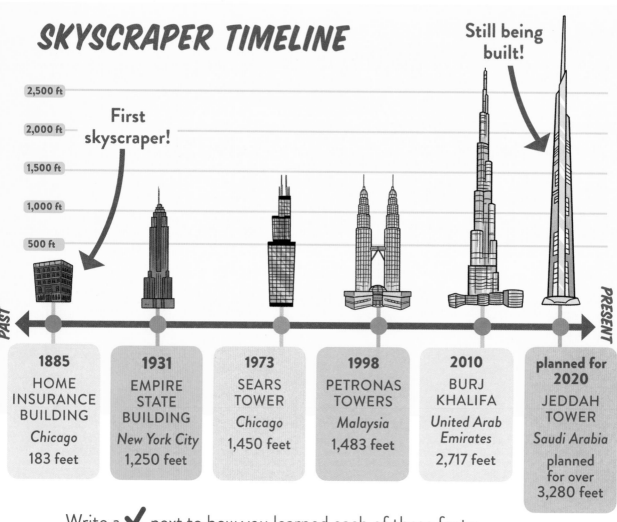

SKYSCRAPER TIMELINE

First skyscraper!

Still being built!

1885	1931	1973	1998	2010	planned for 2020
HOME INSURANCE BUILDING	EMPIRE STATE BUILDING	SEARS TOWER	PETRONAS TOWERS	BURJ KHALIFA	JEDDAH TOWER
Chicago	*New York City*	*Chicago*	*Malaysia*	*United Arab Emirates*	*Saudi Arabia*
183 feet	1,250 feet	1,450 feet	1,483 feet	2,717 feet	planned for over 3,280 feet

Write a ✔ next to how you learned each of these facts: from the text on page 58 or the timeline above.

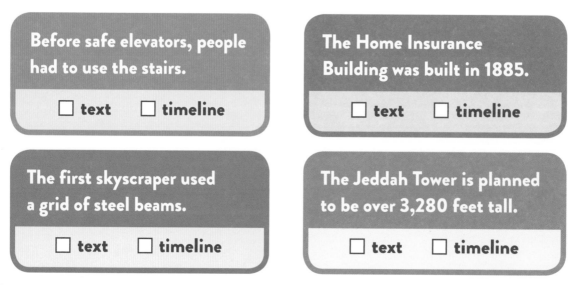

Before safe elevators, people had to use the stairs.

☐ text   ☐ timeline

The Home Insurance Building was built in 1885.

☐ text   ☐ timeline

The first skyscraper used a grid of steel beams.

☐ text   ☐ timeline

The Jeddah Tower is planned to be over 3,280 feet tall.

☐ text   ☐ timeline

Write and draw your own timeline that shows important events from your life.

PAST

Important Events in My Life

Date: _____

_____

_____

_____

_____

_____

Date: _____

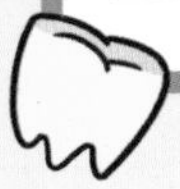

_____

_____

_____

_____

_____

Date: _____

_____

_____

_____

_____

_____

Date: _____

_____

_____

_____

_____

_____

PRESENT

LET'S START! GATHER THESE TOOLS AND MATERIALS.

4 sheets of thick paper

Scissors (with an adult's help)

Glue stick

Heavy book or object

Markers

Optional: pictures of you at different ages

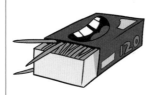
20 or more toothpicks

Clay (or mini marshmallows or grapes)

5 or more rubber bands

LET'S TINKER!

Ask *who, what, where, when, why,* and *how,* to learn more about your materials. Who in your family uses them? What can they be used for? Where are they usually stored? **Ask** other questions using when, why, and how. Can you find a new use for one material by asking questions?

LET'S MAKE: TIMELINE BOOK!

1. Fold 4 sheets of paper in half the long way.

2. Fold each piece in half the other way, and then cut the pages in half on the shorter crease.

3. Arrange the paper V's in a pattern to make mountains and valleys: ∧∨∧∨∧.

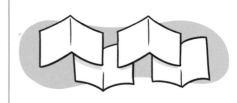

4. Glue the pages together to form an accordion book.

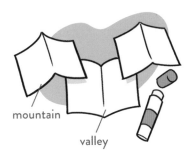

mountain

valley

5. Fold your accordion book and place it under a heavy book or object for a few minutes. This will help it dry flat.

6. Write your name on the cover of your accordion book. Then **number** the pages starting at 1. **Keep writing** until your age!

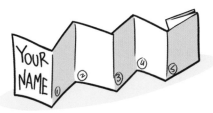

YOUR NAME

7. Glue or draw a picture of you at every age on the matching pages. Then **write** a sentence about your life at that age. Were you a baby? Did you learn to walk? Did you start going to school, or try a new activity?

AGE 5

AGE 5
I PLAYED BASKETBALL!

LET'S ENGINEER!

The skyscrapers in Bungleburg keep wobbling! The builders and engineers of Bungleburg can't seem to keep their skyscrapers standing straight.

How can the MotMots model a stable skyscraper for the Bungleburg engineers?

Design and draw your own skyscraper. Then **use** toothpicks, clay, and rubber bands to build a model. Which design will create the strongest tower? Is it better to use more or fewer toothpicks? Can you build a tower that is taller than a standing up notebook?

PROJECT 8: DONE!
Get your sticker!

Comparing Texts

A **folktale** is a story that has been told over and over. There are often many versions of the same story. Read the two different versions of this folktale aloud.

The Monkey's Heart

A FOLKTALE FROM INDIA

Once upon a time, a monkey lived in a fig tree by a river. One day a hungry crocodile saw the monkey and thought he looked delicious. She wanted to eat his heart! She told her sneaky husband, and he said he'd get the monkey's heart. His wife was confused—the monkey lived in a tree, and the crocodiles lived in the river. How could the monkey be caught?

The next day the sneaky crocodile swam up to the tree and said to the monkey, "On the far side of the river there is a sweet mango tree. I can take you." The monkey liked mangoes, so he hopped on the crocodile's back. In the middle of the river he started to sink. The crocodile snapped, "Sorry, monkey. There is no mango tree. My hungry wife wants to eat your heart!"

Now, the monkey was sneaky, too. "But monkeys don't keep their hearts inside! They would fall out when we climbed trees! I keep my heart in the fig tree," he said. The crocodile took the monkey back to the fig tree to get his heart. The monkey hopped back into the tree and let out a big laugh. "I fooled you, sneaky crocodile! What kind of animal doesn't have a heart inside?"

The Monkey and the Shark

A FOLKTALE FROM AFRICA

There once was a monkey who lived in an apple tree by the ocean. One day the monkey saw a shark in the water below, so he threw some sweet apples down for the shark to eat.

The shark ate the delicious apples. Then he said he'd like to give the monkey a gift, too. He offered the monkey a ride. So the monkey jumped down into the ocean onto the shark's back and went for a ride. In the middle of the trip, the shark said, "I'm sorry, but my king is very sick, so he sent me to get a monkey's heart to heal him."

The monkey was very worried. He thought quickly and said, "Oh dear. I left my heart back at the apple tree!" The shark was confused, so he took the monkey back to the tree. The monkey jumped back into his tree and ran away. No matter what the shark said, he would not come back!

Draw a line to connect each character and event to the correct folktale.

The Monkey's Heart

The Monkey and the Shark

Write and draw to compare
these two folktales.

The Monkey's Heart

Draw the characters in this story.

Draw the setting of this story.

What is one way the endings are the same? Draw one similarity.

How do you think the monkey reacted when the crocodile said,
"My hungry wife wants to eat your heart"? Act it out.

The Monkey and the Shark

Draw the characters in this story.

Draw the setting of this story.

What is one way that the endings are different? Draw one difference.

How do you think the monkey acted when the shark said, "I'm sorry, but my king is very sick, so he sent me to get a monkey's heart to heal him"? Act it out.

Answer each question.

How does the crocodile think he can outsmart the monkey?

_____

_____

_____

_____

How does the shark think he can outsmart the monkey?

_____

_____

_____

_____

How does the monkey outsmart both the shark **and** the crocodile?

_____

_____

_____

_____

What lesson did the crocodile and the shark learn?

_____

_____

_____

_____

A **Venn diagram** can be used to compare similarities and differences between two stories.

Reread the stories on page 66. Then fill in the diagram.

THE MONKEY'S HEART

BOTH STORIES

THE MONKEY AND THE SHARK

<u>The monkey</u>
<u>is the main</u>
<u>character.</u>

<u>The monkey</u>
<u>started to sink.</u>

<u>The shark says</u>
<u>that the king</u>
<u>is sick.</u>

Folktales are told over and over—and often the stories change. Try it! Tell a story to a friend. Have them tell another friend and listen. What changes did you hear?

LET'S START! GATHER THESE TOOLS AND MATERIALS.

Construction paper

Scissors
(with an adult's help)

15 drinking straws

Glue

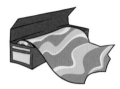
Large piece of foil

Tape

Small rock

LET'S TINKER!

Pick up two of your materials and compare them. What is one way that they are the same? What is one way that they are different? How can you sort your materials based on how they are the same?

LET'S MAKE: MONKEY IN A TREE!

1. Cut a sheet of construction paper in half. On one half of the paper, **make** cuts about 3 inches long on both ends.

2. Fold over the edges of the bottom two pieces, like monkey legs.

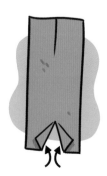

3. Roll the top two pieces around a straw, and use glue to keep them rolled. These are the monkey's arms.

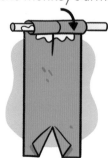

4. Cut a small strip of paper and glue it to the back so that it sticks out like a tail.

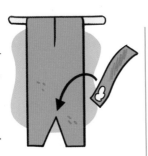

5. Using the other half of the paper, **cut out** 1 large circle and 2 small ones.

6. Get another sheet of paper in a different color and cut out 2 large circles.

7. Glue one large circle onto the middle of the monkey's body.

8. Glue the other 4 circles together to make the monkey's face. **Draw** on eyes and a smile.

9. Hold up the straw to take your monkey for a swing!

LET'S ENGINEER!

The MotMots read the folktales about the clever monkey. Now they want to help monkeys everywhere ride across the ocean or rivers if they want to get mangoes.

How can the MotMots help the monkeys?

Design and build your own vehicle for monkeys to cross water. **Take** the foil, drinking straws, paper, and tape. How can you combine these materials to build a vehicle that will float? **Test** your design in a sink or large bowl of water by putting a small rock on top of your vehicle, like the monkey. Which materials work best? Can you build a boat that floats and keeps the rock dry?

PROJECT 9: DONE!
Get your sticker!

A **script** is the written story for a play, movie, or speech. It contains lines that each character will say and instructions about what the characters should do or act like.

Read the script aloud.

THE LOUD WHISTLE

Zoe is at the park. She is whistling a song. Max walks up to her.

Zoe: Hi, Max! Listen to me whistle!

Zoe puckers her lips and a loud whistle comes out.

Max: Wow! I wish I knew how to do that.

Zoe: I can teach you. First wet your lips. Then pucker them, as if you were making a kissing face. Then blow air through your lips.

Max wets his lips and tries to whistle, but he does not make a sound.

Max: Why isn't it working?

Zoe: I don't know. Try moving your tongue out of the way when you blow.

Max tries again. But he does not make a sound. Xavier walks up.

Max: I just can't whistle. Maybe my mouth isn't small enough. Maybe I'll never be able to whistle at all.

Xavier: Are you trying to whistle? I just learned how. Try this! When you blow air out through your lips, move your mouth and jaw into different positions until you hear a sound.

Max whistles. It's so loud that Zoe and Xavier have to cover their ears!

Max: It worked! Thank you! I'm going to show all my friends.

Max gets up to leave, but Zoe looks confused.

Zoe: What? I couldn't hear what you said. Maybe we should work on whistling quietly next.

Zoe, Max, and Xavier all laugh and whistle a song together.

Create your own ending to the play: What do you think will happen when Max goes to show his friends his new skill? What will Max say and do? What will his friends say and do?

Draw a picture to show what will happen. Then complete the script below.

_____ : _____

_____

_____ : _____

_____

_____ : _____

_____

_____ : _____

_____

Read the play aloud by yourself or with a partner. Try reading it using different voices for the characters.

Read each of the characters' thoughts aloud. Draw a line to connect each thought to the face with the matching emotion.

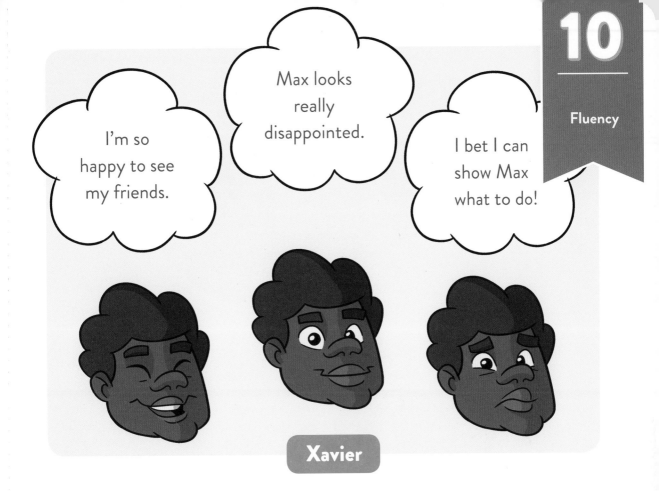

Xavier

Find a partner to play a game:

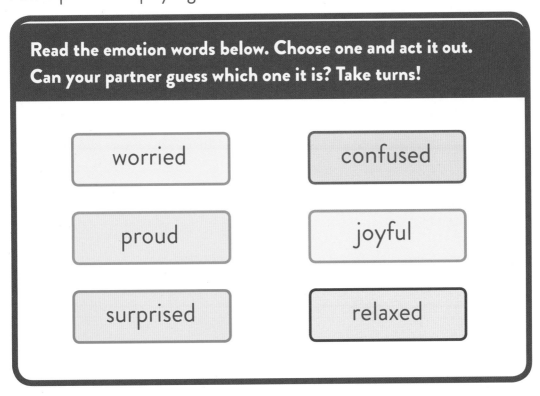

Read the emotion words below. Choose one and act it out. Can your partner guess which one it is? Take turns!

worried	confused
proud	joyful
surprised	relaxed

Write the numbers 1, 2, 3, 4, 5, and 6 to put these events from the play in order from first to last. Then point at each picture in order and retell what happened in the play.

Read the play *The Loud Whistle* again. Think about how Zoe and Xavier tried to teach Max to whistle.

Write about and draw how **you** would teach Max to whistle. (If you can't whistle yet, write about and draw another skill you can teach.)

_____

_____

_____

_____

_____

_____

_____

Share your writing with a friend or family member so someone else can learn, too!

LET'S START!

GATHER THESE TOOLS AND MATERIALS.

4–6 pennies

Marbles

Markers

Toilet paper tube

Paper

Scissors
(with an adult's help)

Drinking straw

A few pieces of grass

LET'S TINKER!

Whistling can make a loud sound. **Use** your materials to see what other sounds you can make! What happens when you tap them, bend them, drop them, or shake them? **Describe** the sounds you hear.

LET'S MAKE: PAPER WHISTLE!

1. Draw this shape about the size of your hand onto a piece of paper.

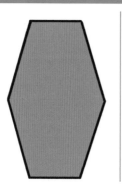

2. Cut it out and fold it in half.

3. Fold over the top edges to make flaps.

4. Cut out a notch.

5. Hold the flaps to your lips and blow!

LET'S ENGINEER!

Dimitri has entered the Tinker Town Whistling Competition. This year the winner will be the MotMot that can whistle in the most ways!

How can Dimitri make a different whistling sound?

Try it yourself! **Wet** your lips and whistle. **Try** flattening the end of a straw and cutting it into a triangle shape. What sounds can you make by blowing into it? Can you whistle by blowing on the side of a piece of grass? Or a leaf? What other materials can you use to make a whistling sound?

PROJECT 10: DONE!
Get your sticker!

Punctuation

The MotMots found a message in a bottle! Read the letter aloud.

To the person who finds this letter,

Ahoy! I'm writing to you from the sea. I sailed away because everyone at home kept calling me a pirate. I got sick of it! They just didn't understand me. My pet parrot stands on my shoulder because he gets lonely. On the way to Bungleburg once, I got sand in my eye. So now I have to wear an eye patch—my mom said so. I also sometimes drop what I am carrying, so I hold a hook in my hand. Why does everyone keep calling me a pirate? Don't they know not to judge a book by its cover? If you are a person who knows that, then I have drawn a map for you. Please keep it a secret!

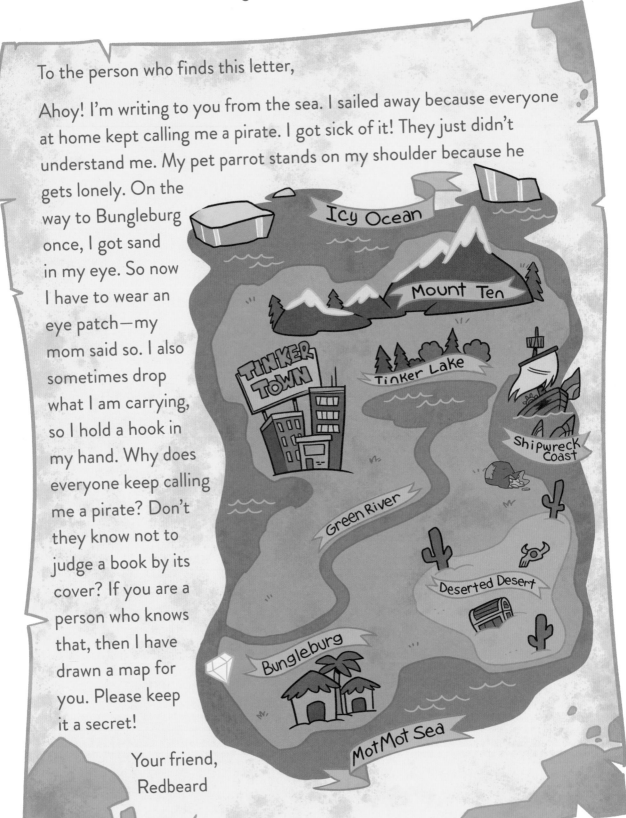

Your friend,
Redbeard

Look at the map to answer each question. Remember that the names of geographic locations should be capitalized.

Where did Redbeard bury his treasure chest?

_____

Draw a **green** line on the map from Tinker Town to the treasure chest. Travel by water past Bungleburg.

Which sea did you sail on?

_____

Which town is closest to the jewels?

_____

Draw a **blue** line on the map from Tinker Lake to the jewels. Travel by river.

Which town has no buried treasure?

_____

Where did Redbeard bury his coins?

_____

Draw a **red** line on the map from Tinker Town to the coins. Travel by water through Icy Ocean.

Which mountain did you pass?

_____

A **possessive noun** uses an apostrophe to show when something belongs to another person or thing.

The MotMots are going on a treasure hunt, and they are each bringing a piece of gear. Look at each picture and write each possessive noun by adding an **'s** after the end of each MotMot's name.

Amelia   **flashlight**

Amelia's flashlight

Callie   **map**

_____

Brian   **compass**

_____

Dimitri   **shovel**

_____

Frank   **snacks**

_____

Enid   **hat**

_____

Look around your home. Use possessive nouns to describe who things belong to.

A **contraction** is a shorter version of a word or words. An apostrophe is used in place of the missing letter or letters.

Replace the underlined words in each sentence with a contraction.

He's		We're		I'm	
Don't	It's		She's		I've

~~We're~~

We are going on a treasure hunt! __We're__

I am very excited. _____

He is going to read the map. _____

She is going to dig. _____

Do not forget the sunscreen! _____

It is going to be a long, hot journey. _____

Uh-oh. I have forgotten the snacks. _____

It's Talk-Like-a-Pirate Day in the MotMots' class.

Fill in the missing punctuation for each of these sentences. Use a **period (.)** for telling sentences, a **question mark (?)** to ask a question, and an **exclamation mark (!)** to share a big feeling, like excitement.

Is Talk-Like-a-Pirate Day real___

Yes, it happens every year on September 19 ___

What happens on that holiday___

Everyone talks like a pirate ___

I think it's the best day of the year___

"Ahoy!" is my favorite thing to say___

I hope I don't have to walk the plank ___

All holidays should be capitalized, like Halloween, Valentine's Day, and Talk-Like-a-Pirate Day!

A **greeting** is the opening of a letter. Common greetings are "Dear Friend," or "Hello!" A **closing** is the ending of a letter. Common closings are "Sincerely," or "Your Friend."

Write a letter to tell a friend about Talk-Like-a-Pirate Day.

Use a comma after the **greeting** here.

Use a comma after the **closing** and write your name below.

LET'S START! GATHER THESE TOOLS AND MATERIALS.

Pencil	Paper	Markers	10 pieces of newspaper	10 small paper bags

Tape	Construction paper	Scissors (with an adult's help)	Glue	Glass or plastic bottle with a lid

LET'S TINKER!

Many words should be capitalized, like people's names, holidays, and geographic locations. The names of products should also be capitalized. **Look** at your materials. Then **brainstorm** and name three of your own products. **Write** the names down, and remember to use capital letters!

LET'S MAKE: 3-D MAP!

1. Crumple a few pieces of newspaper into a ball and put them inside a small paper bag.

2. Fold over the top and tape it closed.

3. **Cut** and glue pieces of construction paper to add details to make the paper bag look like your home. **Add** doors, windows, and a roof.

4. **Repeat** steps 1 through 3 to make other buildings in your town, including your school, a store, and a friend's home.

5. **Cut** other shapes from construction paper to add more details to your map, like roads, a field, or a pond.

6. **Place** the buildings and other items where they belong on the floor—some may be close to your home and some may be far.

LET'S ENGINEER!

The MotMots are thinking about when they'll be grown up. They wonder what it will be like! But they don't want to forget who they are today.

How can the MotMots record their favorite things and facts about themselves, and save them for the future?

Make your own message in a bottle. **Wash** and dry the inside of your empty bottle. What can you put inside that shares details about yourself? **Close** the bottle tightly when you are done. **Find** a place to store it until you are graduating third grade. Then **open** it up!

PROJECT 11: DONE!
Get your sticker!

Writing Sentences

A **diagram** uses drawings and designs to share information so that it is easy to read and understand. Read the diagram aloud. Start at the top and follow the arrows.

Most mother frogs lay their **eggs** underwater to keep them wet. Some types of frogs lay over 1,000 eggs at a time.

FROG LIFE CYCLE

A **tadpole** hatches from each egg. The tadpoles have long tails and live underwater. As they grow, legs and arms develop.

Froglets keep growing into **frogs**. Frogs have no tails. They can breathe air and live in the water and on land.

Tadpoles grow into **froglets**. Their gills change into lungs for breathing on land. Their tails shrink and they climb out of the water.

Look closely at each picture to find the difference and circle the one described. Then complete the sentence. Use a **period (.)** to end each sentence.

One tadpole is ready to hatch. It will live under the

_____

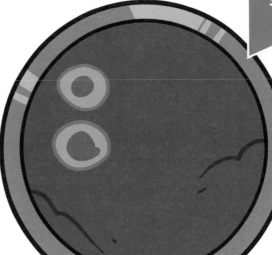

One tadpole has grown

_____

One froglet is using his legs to climb

_____

_____

_____

Have you ever seen a tadpole? What other animals and their babies have you seen around your home?

Look at each picture and write a sentence about what you observe. Use a capital letter to begin each sentence, and end each sentence with the correct punctuation.

Read each set of facts. Write one compound sentence that includes both facts. Use a comma and a conjunction word, like **and**, **but**, or **so**.

FACTS

Most frogs are carnivorous. They eat other small animals.

Most frogs are carnivorous,
so they eat other small animals.

FACTS

Frogs get water through their skin. They do not drink water.

_____

_____

FACTS

Some types of frogs live in trees. Others live underground.

_____

_____

Read this compound sentence. Then write the two facts as separate sentences.

Frogs do not have ears that you can see, but they can hear well.

FACT # 1 _____

FACT # 2 _____

Write a sentence about what you think each frog will do next.

glass frog

_____

_____

_____

ghost frog

_____

_____

_____

flying frog

_____

_____

_____

leaf frog

_____

_____

_____

Look at the pictures. Then write a sentence in each thought bubble to show what the frogs are thinking. Last, give the story a title and read it aloud.

TITLE: _____

LET'S START! GATHER THESE TOOLS AND MATERIALS.

3 or more craft sticks

Construction paper

Scissors
(with an adult's help)

Glue

Optional: A few small
round objects
(like pom-poms or buttons)

Index card

Markers or crayons

Paper plate

LET'S TINKER!

Use your materials to make thought bubbles. Then **write** sentences on them to show what you are thinking.

LET'S MAKE: JUMPING FROG!

1. Fold over the top corners of an index card. Then **open** it back up.

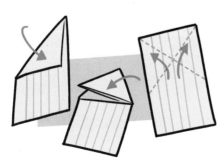

2. Use two fingers to pull in the sides, and press the top triangle flat.

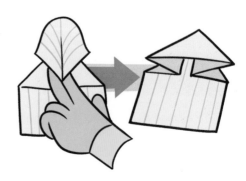

3. Fold the two edges of the triangle up to the top. These make the frog's front legs!

4. Fold in the leftover sides to meet in the middle.

5. Fold the bottom up. Then **fold** the top layer back to form the frog's back legs.

6. Color and add details to your frog. Then **push** down with your finger to watch it jump!

LET'S ENGINEER!

The MotMots are studying the life cycle of frogs, and are thinking about their own life cycles. They've changed a lot since they were baby MotMots!

How can the MotMots make models of their own life cycles?

Use your materials to make a model of your own life cycle. How can you show what you looked like as a baby? What you look like now? And what you might look like when you grow up and when you're old? **Write** a sentence about each part of your life cycle. How have you changed?

PROJECT 12: DONE!
Get your sticker!

Telling a Story

A **biography** is a story about a person's life, written by someone else. Read this biography aloud.

Jane Goodall

Jane Goodall is an English scientist who studied chimpanzees. She became interested in animals when she was very young. She kept a journal with notes and drawings about the animals she saw around her home, like chickens, insects, and worms.

When she was twenty-six years old she went to Tanzania, a country in Africa. She went there to live with chimpanzees so she could study them—something no one had done before! At first, when she tried to watch them, they would run away. But she kept trying. She'd stand far away and watch them eat. After a while, they got used to her being around.

Just like when she was young, Jane kept notes in her journal. She wrote down what the chimpanzees did, where they went, and how they acted. It took a whole year, but the chimpanzees got used to her and let her get closer. After another year they were no longer afraid. She got to know them and gave them all names. She spent time living in the trees with them and even ate their food with them.

From watching the chimpanzees closely, Jane learned things about them that no one else had ever discovered. They had families and relationships. They gave hugs! They used different sounds like a language to talk to each other. They sometimes ate meat, like insects and birds. They used sticks as tools and threw stones as weapons.

Jane became famous for her work studying chimpanzees. Her important discoveries helped scientists all over the world. She used her notes to write many books. Today, she still talks to people about chimpanzees—she teaches others about what chimpanzees need and how people can protect them.

Write a ✔ next to the event that happened FIRST.

☐ Jane went to Tanzania.

☐ Jane gave the chimpanzees names.

Write a ✔ next to the event that happened FIRST.

☐ Jane made new discoveries about chimpanzees.

☐ The chimpanzees ran away from Jane.

How did Jane use her journal when she was YOUNG?

_____

_____

_____

Draw a picture of what you think a page of Jane's journal may have looked like when she was an ADULT.

Jane Goodall kept a journal to record notes from her days with the chimpanzees. Write to record your own events and memories.

Write about something you did today. How did you feel?

_____

_____

_____

_____

Write about a place you like to go. How far away is it?

_____

_____

_____

_____

Write about one way you travel around your town. What do you see on your trips?

_____

_____

_____

Write about someone in your family. What do you do together?

_____

_____

_____

_____

Write about something you like to do. What is the best part?

_____

_____

_____

_____

Write about a time you saw a friend. What did you say?

_____

_____

_____

_____

A biography is a story about a person's life, written by someone else. An autobiography is written by an author about his or her own life.

Write and draw your autobiography. Use the events and memories on pages 100–101 to help you.

MY AUTOBIOGRAPHY

Written by: _____

_____

_____

_____

_____

_____

_____

_____

_____

_____

_____

_____

There are many digital tools available to share your writing—computers, tablets, phones, and more. Ask an adult to help you share your story with a friend or family member who is far away.

LET'S START!

GATHER THESE TOOLS AND MATERIALS.

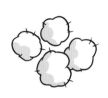
Cotton balls

String

Glue

Pencil

Paper

3 paper bags

Hole punch

Scissors
(with an adult's help)

Old magazines

LET'S TINKER!

When Jane Goodall was young, she wrote notes and drew sketches of the animals she saw around her home. **Use** your materials to make pictures of the animals you see around your home. Do any live inside? Which ones do you see outside? Are there any you wish could live inside with you?

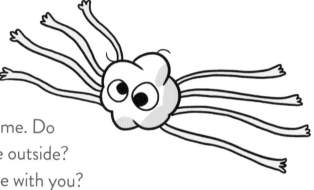

LET'S MAKE: POCKET JOURNAL!

1. Fold the bottom of 3 paper bags over, and glue each in place.

2. Then **fold** each of the 3 bags in half.

3. Take one bag and punch 2 holes along the fold.

4. Use that bag as a guide to mark the other 2 bags in the same place with a pencil. Then **punch** holes in both of them.

5. With the help of an adult, **cut** a 2-foot piece of string. **Stack** the 3 folded bags so that all the holes line up, like a book. **Wrap** the string through the holes many times and tie it in the back.

6. Now you can **write** in your journal, and store things in the pockets!

LET'S ENGINEER!

Brian likes to write in a journal like Jane Goodall. He uses it to jot down memories and stories about his life. Today he wants to add some pictures to his journal, but he only has scissors and glue.

How can he make pictures that help him tell his stories?

Choose a story that you want to tell. **Use** the materials to make a collage that tells the story! **Cut** and glue pictures from magazines, newspapers, or photographs. How can you show what you did? And what you said? And how you felt?

PROJECT 13: DONE!
Get your sticker!

Writing Informational Texts

Read the instructions aloud.

How to Tie Your Shoes

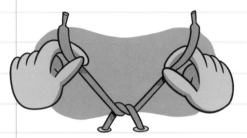

First, cross your laces.

Next, make two big loops.

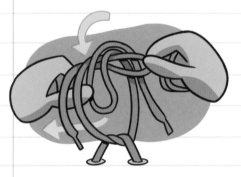

Then, cross the loops and tuck one under the other.

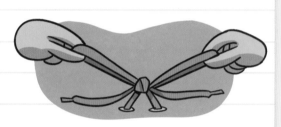

Last, pull the loops tight!

Circle the step that comes first.

 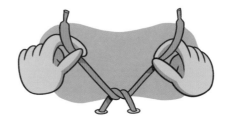

What do you think would happen if you skipped this step?

_____

_____

_____

Circle the step that comes last.

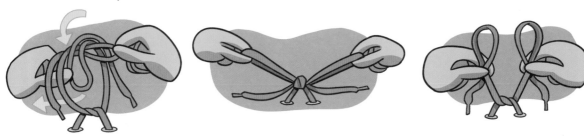

What do you think would happen if you skipped this step?

_____

_____

_____

Are there any steps that you think could be skipped? Why or why not?

_____

_____

Read the instructions again. Can you
follow the steps to tie your own shoes?

Write and draw to fill in the missing steps in each set of instructions.

How to Make a Jelly Sandwich

First, get 2 pieces of bread, a jar of jelly, and a spoon.

Next, put a spoonful of jelly on a piece of bread and spread it.

Last, _____

_____

_____

_____

How to Brush Your Teeth

First, squeeze toothpaste onto your toothbrush.

Next, _____

_____

_____

_____

Last, _____

_____

_____

_____

Brainstorm topics that you are an expert on and could teach someone else how to do. Then write and draw them in the chart.

I am an expert on:

Choose one of the topics you are an expert on from page 109. Write your own instructions below. Add drawings to show details.

HOW TO _____

_____

First, _____

_____

Next, _____

_____

Then, _____

_____

Last, _____

_____

Share your instructions with a friend or family member and follow the steps together!

LET'S START!

20 craft sticks

10 paper or plastic cups

LET'S TINKER!

Combine and stack your craft sticks and cups to see what you can build. **Share** your design with a friend or family member. **Tell** them the steps you took to build your design. Then **let** them have a turn to build. What steps did they take? **Talk** about your different designs.

LET'S MAKE: CRAFT STICK SNAPPER!

1. Stack 2 craft sticks to make a V shape.

2. Add another craft stick on top, in the middle.

3. Carefully **place** your fourth stick *on top* of the middle stick, but *under* the side sticks.

4. Wiggle the fifth stick *under* the middle stick, but *on top* of the side sticks. (The secret of the snapper is that the sticks are held together with tension—each stick pushes and pulls on the others. This can make it tricky to build your first time. Work with a friend or family member until you get the hang of building it yourself.)

5. Drop your snapper and watch it snap apart!

LET'S ENGINEER!

It's Tinker Town's annual Snapper Contest! Last year, Enid made a V-shaped snapper and won! Now, she must defend her trophy.

How can she build a new unique design for a snapper?

Experiment with the instructions above to design your own craft stick snapper. Can you make one with more sticks? What about fewer? Can you make one that is stronger? Or flies farther? Or one that snaps higher when it drops? What other materials can be added? **Write** or draw instructions for how to make your own snapper design.

PROJECT 14: DONE!
Get your sticker!

Writing Your Opinion

Opinions are someone's thoughts, feelings, or beliefs about something. They are not based on facts, and may not be true. Read each opinion essay aloud.

EMMA

I think that losing teeth is the best! I lost my first tooth yesterday at bedtime, and now I cannot wait to lose more teeth. It fell out while I was reading a book. One minute, I was wiggling it in my mouth, and the next minute, it was in my hand. I jumped out of bed to show my mom. My family was so happy—we had a tooth party! And soon, I'll get an even bigger adult tooth in the same spot.

ALEX

I think that losing teeth is gross. I have lost three teeth so far. All three have fallen out at school while I was eating apples at lunch! Everyone at my lunch table said, "Ew!"—even me. My teacher said I should bring bananas instead.

I do not like the feeling of loose teeth because they move around in my mouth. Also, wiggly teeth make it hard to eat. I hope it is a long time before I lose another tooth.

Circle the face that shows how each character felt about losing a tooth.

EMMA

ALEX

? What reasons did the characters give to explain their opinions?

EMMA:

_____

_____

_____

ALEX:

_____

_____

_____

? Write a question you want to ask each character to learn more about their opinions.

EMMA:

_____

_____

_____

ALEX:

_____

_____

_____

Write about and draw your own memories of losing teeth.

How old were you when you lost your first tooth? _____

Where were you when it fell out? _____

If you haven't lost a tooth, how old do you think you will be when you do lose your first tooth? Why?

_____

_____

Draw a picture of what happened when you lost your most recent tooth.

(Or draw what you think might happen.)

What do you do with your teeth after they fall out?

(Or draw what you will do.)

_____

_____

How many teeth have you lost in all? _____

Research other people's opinions. Ask friends or family members the questions below and write their thoughts and opinions.

Name: _____

When did you lose your first tooth? _____

What was it like? _____

_____

How did you feel about it? _____

_____

Name: _____

When did you lose your first tooth? _____

What was it like? _____

_____

How did you feel about it? _____

_____

Write about and draw how you feel about losing teeth.

I feel . . . _____

_____

Because . . . _____

_____

_____

Also . . . _____

_____

_____

Another reason I feel
this way is . . .

_____

_____

_____

Write your own opinion essay about losing teeth. Provide reasons for why you think and feel that way. Use the events and memories on page 118 to help you. Include a closing that sums up your opinion.

TITLE: _____

_____

_____

_____

_____

_____

_____

_____

_____

_____

_____

_____

LET'S START!

GATHER THESE TOOLS AND MATERIALS.

 4 clothespins	 Markers	 Glue	 Construction paper	 Scissors (with an adult's help)
 Apple	 Knife (with an adult's help)	 Nut butter or honey	 Mini marshmallows	White beans (dried)

LET'S TINKER!

Use markers to draw faces and teeth on 4 clothespins. You can also **add** cut paper with glue. Which is your favorite? Which is the funniest? Are any of them scary?

Talk about your opinions with a friend or family member. **Ask** what their opinions are.

LET'S MAKE: TOOTHY SNACK!

1. With the help of an adult, **cut** an apple into slices.

2. Spread nut butter (or honey) on the top of two slices.

3. Line up marshmallows on top of the nut butter on one of the apple slices.

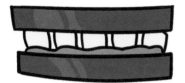

4. Lay the other apple slice on top, with the nut butter facing down like glue.

5. Follow the directions again to make another one to share!

LET'S ENGINEER!

Callie loves teeth. She likes chewing with them, counting them, and even losing them. But most of all, she likes getting new ones! Her mouth is always changing as teeth fall out and new ones come in. Callie wants to remember what her smile looks like right now.

How can she make a model of which teeth are in her mouth, and which are not?

Use your beans to make a model of the teeth in your mouth. How can you figure out how many teeth are in your mouth? How can you show which teeth are missing in your model? Can you show which are new larger adult teeth and which are still baby teeth?

PROJECT 15: DONE!
Get your sticker!

ANSWER KEY

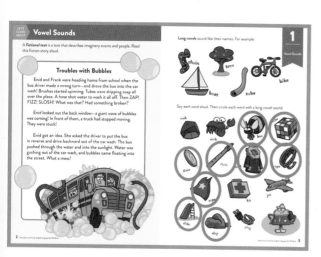

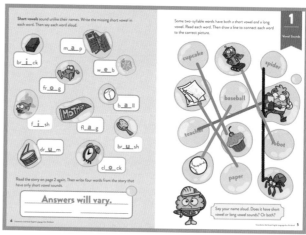

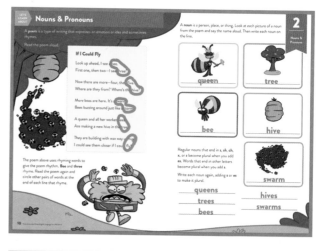

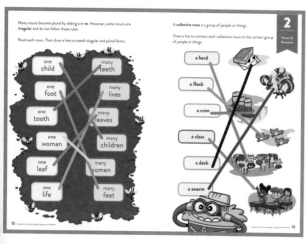

Verbs, Adverbs & Adjectives — 3

TINKER TOWN NEWS

NEW ICE CREAM SHOP IS COOL

Read the newspaper article aloud.

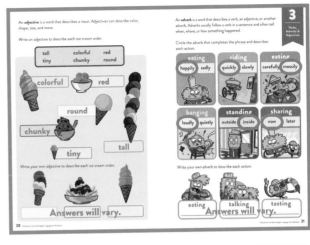

Verbs are action words that can tell what happened in the past, present, or future. Rewrite the verb in each sentence in the past tense.

Amelia rides to the store.
Amelia **rode** to the store.

Enid sees the sign!
Enid **saw** the sign!

Brian feels excited.
Brian **felt** excited.

Dimitri sits at a table.
Dimitri **sat** at a table.

Frank gives his order.
Frank **gave** his order.

Callie eats ice cream.
Callie **ate** ice cream.

Look at what each MotMot is thinking about. Then write what each one may be thinking. Use the adjectives from the word bank to add details.

Word bank: cold fluffy sweet giant chocolaty

Answers will vary.

Draw the ice cream you would order! Then write adjectives to describe it.

Answers will vary.

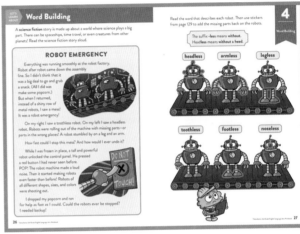

An **adjective** is a word that describes a noun. Adjectives can describe color, shape, size, and more.

Write an adjective to describe each ice cream order.

Word bank: tall colorful red tiny chunky round

colorful red round chunky tiny tall

Write your own adjective to describe each ice cream order.

Answers will vary.

An **adverb** is a word that describes a verb, an adjective, or another adverb. Adverbs usually follow a verb in a sentence and often tell when, where, or how something happened.

Circle the adverb that completes the phrase and describes each action.

eating: happily / sadly
riding: quickly / slowly
eating: carefully / messily
banging: loudly / quietly
standing: outside / inside
sharing: now / later

Write your own adverb to describe each action.

eating talking tasting
Answers will vary.

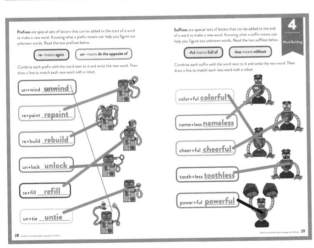

Word Building — 4

Prefixes are special sets of letters that can be added to the start of a word to make a new word. Knowing what a prefix means can help you figure out unknown words. Read the two prefixes below.

re- means **again**   **un-** means **do the opposite of**

Combine each prefix with the word next to it and write the new word. Then draw a line to match each new word with a robot.

un+wind **unwind**
re+paint **repaint**
re+build **rebuild**
un+lock **unlock**
re+fill **refill**
un+tie **untie**

Suffixes are special sets of letters that can be added to the end of a word to make a new word. Knowing what a suffix means can help you figure out unknown words. Read the two suffixes below.

-ful means **full of**   **-less** means **without**

Combine each suffix with the word next to it and write the new word. Then draw a line to match each new word with a robot.

color+ful **colorful**
name+less **nameless**
cheer+ful **cheerful**
tooth+less **toothless**
power+ful **powerful**

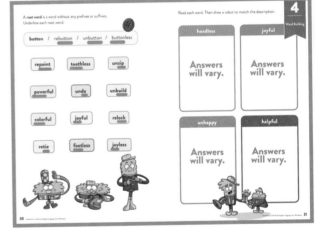

A **root word** is a word without any prefixes or suffixes. Underline each root word.

button / rebutton / unbutton / buttonless
repaint toothless unzip
powerful undo unbuild
colorful joyful relock
retie footless joyless

Read each word. Then draw a robot to match the description.

headless — Answers will vary.
joyful — Answers will vary.
unhappy — Answers will vary.
helpful — Answers will vary.

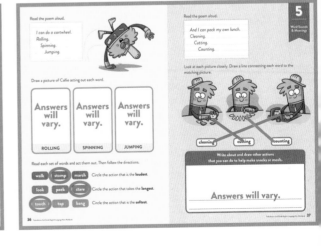

Word Building — 4

A **science fiction** story is made up about a world where science plays a big part. There can be spaceships, time travel, or even creatures from other planets! Read the science fiction story aloud.

ROBOT EMERGENCY

Read the word that describes each robot. Then use stickers from page 129 to add the missing parts back on the robots.

The suffix **-less** means without. Headless means without a head.

headless armless legless
toothless footless noseless

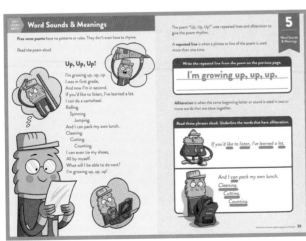

Word Sounds & Meanings — 5

Free verse poems have no patterns or rules. They don't even have to rhyme.

Read the poem aloud.

Up, Up, Up!

I'm growing up, up, up.
I was in first grade,
And now I'm in second.
If you'd like to listen, I've learned a lot.
I can do a cartwheel.
Rolling.
Spinning.
Jumping.
And I can pack my own lunch.
Cleaning.
Cutting.
Counting.
I can even tie my shoes,
All by myself.
What will I be able to do next?
I'm growing up, up, up!

The poem "Up, Up, Up!" uses repeated lines and alliteration to give the poem rhythm.

A **repeated line** is when a phrase or line of the poem is used more than one time.

Write the repeated line from the poem on the previous page.

I'm growing up, up, up.

Alliteration is when the same beginning letter or sound is used in two or more words that are close together.

Read these phrases aloud. Underline the words that have alliteration.

If you'd like to listen, I've learned a lot.

And I can pack my own lunch.
Cleaning.
Cutting.
Counting.

Word Sounds & Meanings — 5

Read the poem aloud.

I can do a cartwheel.
Rolling.
Spinning.
Jumping.

Draw a picture of Callie acting out each word.

Answers will vary. Answers will vary. Answers will vary.
ROLLING SPINNING JUMPING

And I can pack my own lunch.
Cleaning.
Cutting.
Counting.

Look at each picture closely. Draw a line connecting each word to the matching picture.

cleaning cutting counting

Write about and draw other actions that you can do to help make snacks or meals.

Answers will vary.

Read each set of words and act them out. Then follow the directions.

walk stomp march — Circle the action that is the loudest.
look peek stare — Circle the action that takes the longest.
touch tap bang — Circle the action that is the softest.

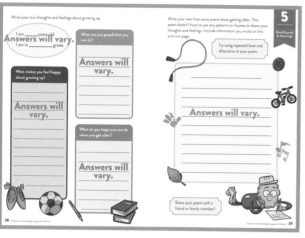

Write your own thoughts and feelings about growing up.

I am _____ years old.
I am in _____ grade.
Answers will vary.

What are you proud that you can do?
Answers will vary.

What makes you feel happy about growing up?
Answers will vary.

What do you hope you can do when you get older?
Answers will vary.

Write your own free verse poem about getting older. This poem doesn't have to use any patterns or rhymes to share your thoughts and feelings. Include information you wrote on the previous page.

Try using repeated lines and alliteration in your poem.

Answers will vary.

Share your poem with a friend or family member!

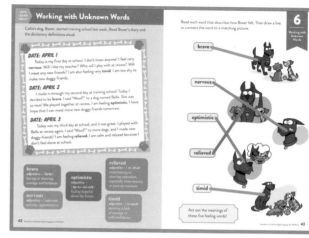

Working with Unknown Words

Callie's dog, Boxer, started training school last week. Read Boxer's diary and the dictionary definitions aloud.

DATE: APRIL 1
Today is my first day at school. I don't know anyone! I feel very **nervous**. Will I like my teacher? Who will I play with at recess? Will I meet any new friends? I am also feeling very **timid**. I am too shy to make new doggy friends.

DATE: APRIL 2
I made it through my second day at training school! Today I decided to be **brave**. I said "Woof!" to a dog named Bella. She was so nice! We played together at recess. I am feeling **optimistic**. I have hope that I can meet more new doggy friends tomorrow.

DATE: APRIL 3
Today was my third day at school, and it was great. I played with Bella at recess again. I said "Woof!" to more dogs, and I made new doggy friends! I am feeling **relieved**. I am calm and relaxed because I don't feel alone at school.

Read each word that describes how Boxer felt. Then draw a line to connect the word to a matching picture.

brave
nervous
optimistic
relieved
timid

brave adjective – \bräv\ having or showing courage and boldness

optimistic adjective – \äp-tə-mi-stik\ feeling hopeful about the future

nervous adjective – \nər-vəs\ anxious, apprehensive

relieved adjective – \ri-lēvd\ experiencing or showing relaxation, especially from anxiety or pent-up emotions

timid adjective – \ti-məd\ showing a lack of courage or self-confidence

Act out the meanings of these five feeling words!

Read each sentence aloud, and look at each underlined word. Circle the word below each sentence that means the same thing.

I had **chunky** muffins with pieces of fruit inside.
smooth / lumpy

At school we have to eat fast because lunchtime is **brief**.
short / long

They tasted so **superb** that I ate all five!
awful / great

I wanted to be **gutsy**, so I said "Woof!" to more new dogs.
shy / brave

They were so **puny** that five fit in my paw.
tiny / large

Bella couldn't eat her whole muffin because it was too **massive**.
big / small

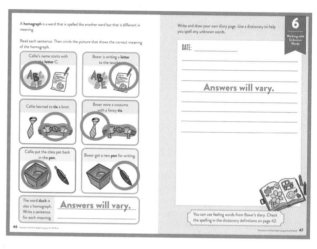

A **homograph** is a word that is spelled like another word but that is different in meaning.

Read each sentence. Then circle the picture that shows the correct meaning of the homograph.

Callie's name starts with the **letter** C.
Boxer is writing a **letter** to the teacher.

Callie learned to **tie** a knot.
Boxer wore a costume with a fancy **tie**.

Callie put the class pet back in the **pen**.
Boxer got a new **pen** for writing.

The word **duck** is also a homograph. Write a sentence for each meaning.
Answers will vary.

Write and draw your own diary page. Use a dictionary to help you spell any unknown words.

DATE: _____
Answers will vary.

You can use feeling words from Boxer's diary. Check the spelling in the dictionary definitions on page 42.

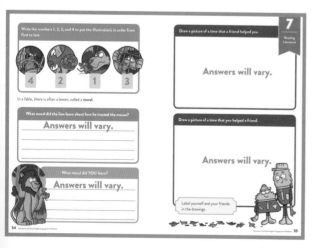

Reading Literature

A **fable** is a short made-up story that often uses talking animals to teach a lesson. There is usually a hero and a villain in the story. Read the fable aloud.

The Lion and the Mouse

One day a mouse was playing in the bright, leafy woods. He raced down tall trees and jumped over logs. He was running so fast that he ran right into the nose of a sleeping lion! The lion woke up and caught the tiny mouse with his giant paw. The mouse shook with fear. "Please let me go! If you help me, someday I will help you," he begged. The lion let out a huge roaring laugh. Someone so tiny could never help him! He got such a good laugh that he decided to be kind and let the mouse go.

Later, the lion was roaming the woods. SWOOSH! He accidentally stepped into a trap hidden by a hunter. A net lifted him off the ground—he was stuck. "HELP!" he roared at the top of his lungs.

The mouse heard the roaring from far away and ran through the branches as fast as he could. When he got to the lion, he jumped up and started chewing the net. In a few minutes he chewed through the rope and set the lion free! "You laughed at me," the mouse reminded the lion. "You said that a mouse could never help a lion. But now you know! You can't judge what someone can do by how they look. Even someone tiny can be a giant hero."

Read the fable again. Try using different voices for the characters.

Write a ✔ next to why the mouse ran into the lion.
☐ He was running too fast.
☐ He wanted to meet the lion.
☐ He had stepped into a trap.

Circle how the mouse felt when the lion caught him.

Circle how the lion felt when the mouse promised he would help the lion.

Write a word you would use to describe this feeling:
Answers will vary.

Write a word you would use to describe this feeling:
Answers will vary.

Write a ✔ next to what the lion did to the mouse.
☐ He kept the mouse.
☐ He let the mouse go.
☐ He asked the mouse to help him someday.

Write a ✔ next to why the lion stepped into a trap.
☐ The trap was made of rope.
☐ The trap was gone.
☐ The trap was hidden.

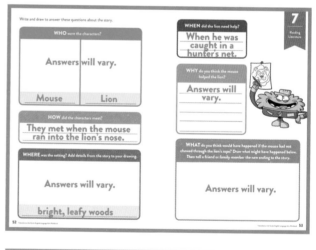

Write and draw to answer these questions about the story.

WHO were the characters?
Answers will vary.
Mouse | Lion

HOW did the characters meet?
They met when the mouse ran into the lion's nose.

WHERE was the setting? Add details from the story to your drawing.
Answers will vary.
bright, leafy woods

WHEN did the lion need help?
When he was caught in a hunter's net.

WHY do you think the mouse helped the lion?
Answers will vary.

WHAT do you think would have happened if the mouse had not chewed through the lion's rope? Draw what might have happened below. Then tell a friend or family member the new ending to the story.
Answers will vary.

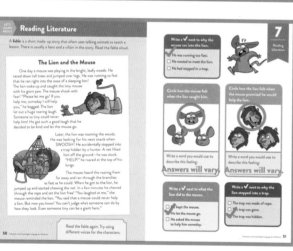

Write the numbers 1, 2, 3, and 4 to put the illustrations in order from first to last.

4 2 1 3

In a fable, there is often a lesson, called a **moral**.

What moral did the lion learn about how he trusted the mouse?
Answers will vary.

What moral did YOU learn?
Answers will vary.

Draw a picture of a time that a friend helped you.
Answers will vary.

Draw a picture of a time that you helped a friend.
Answers will vary.

Label yourself and your friends in the drawings.

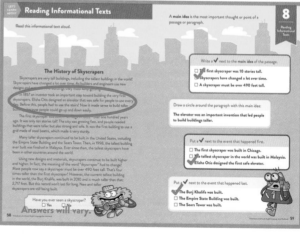

Reading Informational Texts

Read this informational text aloud.

The History of Skyscrapers

Skyscrapers are very tall buildings, including the tallest buildings in the world! Skyscrapers have changed a lot over time. As builders and engineers use new designs and materials, skyscrapers continue to get taller.

In 1857 an inventor took an important step toward building the very first skyscraper. Elisha Otis designed an elevator that was safe for people to use every day. Before this, people had to use the stairs! Now it made sense to build taller, because people could go up and down easily.

The first skyscrapers were built in the United States about one hundred years ago. It was only ten stories tall! The city was growing fast, and people needed buildings that were taller but also strong and safe. It was the first building to use a grid made of steel beams, which made it very sturdy.

Many taller skyscrapers continued to be built in the United States, including the Empire State Building and the Sears Tower. Then, in 1998, the tallest building ever built was finished in Malaysia. Ever since then, the tallest skyscrapers have been in other countries around the world.

Using new designs and materials, skyscrapers continue to be built higher and higher. In fact, the design of "skyscrapers" had to change! Most people now say a skyscraper must be over 490 feet tall. That's four times taller than the first skyscraper! However, the current tallest building in the world, the Burj Khalifa, was built in 2010 and is much taller than that: 2,717 feet. But this record won't last for long. New and taller skyscrapers are still being built.

Have you ever seen a skyscraper?
☐ Yes ☐ No
Answers will vary.

A **main idea** is the most important thought or point of a passage or paragraph.

Write a ✔ next to the **main idea** of the passage.
☐ The first skyscraper was 10 stories tall.
☑ Skyscrapers have changed a lot over time.
☐ A skyscraper must be over 490 feet tall.

Draw a circle around the paragraph with this main idea:
The elevator was an important invention that led people to build buildings taller.

Put a 1 next to the event that happened first.
☐ The first skyscraper was built in Chicago.
☐ The tallest skyscraper in the world was built in Malaysia.
☐ Elisha Otis designed the first safe elevator.

Put a 4 next to the event that happened last.
☑ The Burj Khalifa was built.
☐ The Empire State Building was built.
☐ The Sears Tower was built.

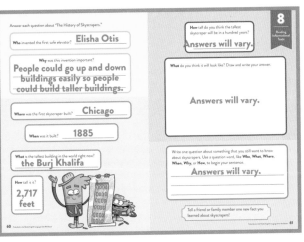

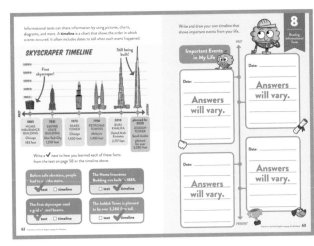

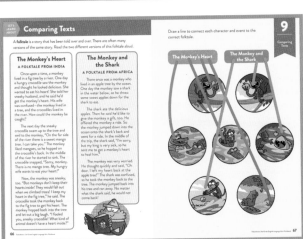

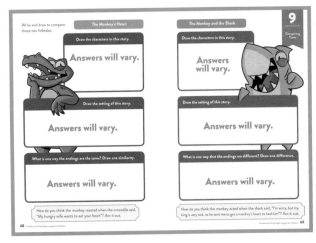

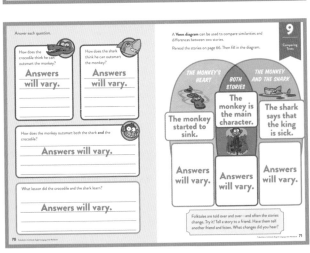

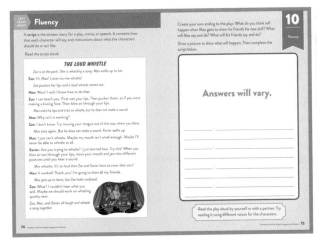

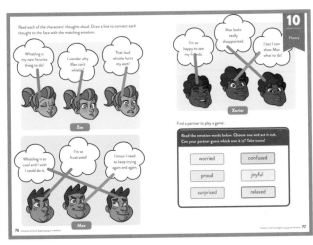

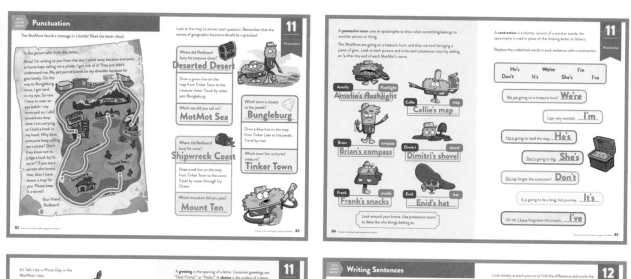

Punctuation

The MotMots found a message in a bottle! Read the letter aloud.

To the person who finds this letter,

Ahoy! I'm writing to you from the sea. I sailed away because everyone at home kept calling me a pirate. I got sick of it! They just didn't understand me. My pet parrot stands on my shoulder because he gets lonely. On the way to Bungleburg once, I got sand in my eye. So now I have to wear an eye patch—my mom said so. I also sometimes drop what I am carrying, so I hold a hook in my hand. Why does everyone keep calling me a pirate? Don't they know not to judge a book by its cover? If you are a person who knows that, then I have drawn a map for you. Please keep it a secret!

Your friend,
Redbeard

Look at the map to answer each question. Remember that the names of geographic locations should be capitalized.

Where did Redbeard bury his treasure chest?
Deserted Desert

Draw a green line on the map from Tinker Town to the treasure chest. Travel by water past Bungleburg.

Which sea did you sail on?
MotMot Sea

Which town is closest to the jewels?
Bungleburg

Draw a blue line on the map from Tinker Lake to the jewels. Travel by river.

Where did Redbeard bury his coins?
Shipwreck Coast

Which town has no buried treasure?
Tinker Town

Draw a red line on the map from Tinker Town to the coins. Travel by water through Icy Ocean.

Which mountain did you pass?
Mount Ten

A **possessive noun** uses an apostrophe to show when something belongs to another person or thing.

The MotMots are going on a treasure hunt, and they are each bringing a piece of gear. Look at each picture and write each possessive noun by adding an 's after the end of each MotMot's name.

Amelia — flashlight
Amelia's flashlight

Callie — map
Callie's map

Brian — compass
Brian's compass

Dimitri — shovel
Dimitri's shovel

Frank — snacks
Frank's snacks

Enid — hat
Enid's hat

Look around your home. Use possessive nouns to describe who things belong to.

A **contraction** is a shorter version of a word or words. An apostrophe is used in place of the missing letter or letters.

Replace the underlined words in each sentence with a contraction.

He's   We're   I'm
Don't   It's   She's   I've

We are going on a treasure hunt! **We're**

I am very excited. **I'm**

He is going to read the map. **He's**

She is going to dig. **She's**

Do not forget the sunscreen! **Don't**

It is going to be a long, hot journey. **It's**

Uh-oh. I have forgotten the snacks. **I've**

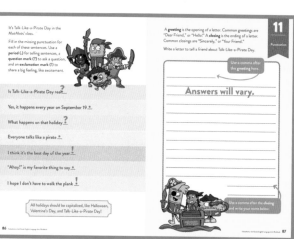

It's Talk-Like-a-Pirate Day in the MotMots' class.

Fill in the missing punctuation for each of these sentences. Use a **period** (.) for telling sentences, a **question mark** (?) to ask a question, and an **exclamation mark** (!) to share a big feeling, like excitement.

Is Talk-Like-a-Pirate Day real **?**

Yes, it happens every year on September 19 **.**

What happens on that holiday **?**

Everyone talks like a pirate **.**

I think it's the best day of the year **!**

"Ahoy!" is my favorite thing to say **.**

I hope I don't have to walk the plank **!**

All holidays should be capitalized, like Halloween, Valentine's Day, and Talk-Like-a-Pirate Day!

A **greeting** is the opening of a letter. Common greetings are "Dear Friend," or "Hello." A **closing** is the ending of a letter. Common closings are "Sincerely," or "Your Friend."

Write a letter to tell a friend about Talk-Like-a-Pirate Day.

Use a comma after the greeting here.

Answers will vary.

Use a comma after the closing and write your name below.

Writing Sentences

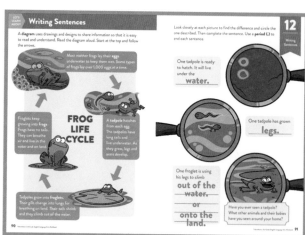

A **diagram** uses drawings and designs to share information so that it is easy to read and understand. Read the diagram aloud. Start at the top and follow the arrows.

FROG LIFE CYCLE

Most mother frogs lay their eggs underwater to keep them wet. Some types of frogs lay over 1,000 eggs at a time.

A **tadpole** hatches from each egg. The tadpoles have long tails and live underwater. As they grow, legs and arms develop.

Tadpoles grow into froglets. Their gills change into lungs for breathing on land. Their tails shrink and they climb out of the water.

Froglets keep growing into frogs. Frogs have no tails. They can breathe air and live in the water and on land.

Look closely at each picture to find the difference and circle the one described. Then complete the sentence. Use a **period** (.) to end each sentence.

One tadpole is ready to hatch. It will live under the **water.**

One tadpole has grown **legs.**

One froglet is using his legs to climb **out of the water,** or **onto the land.**

Have you ever seen a tadpole? What other animals and their babies have you seen around your home?

Look at each picture and write a sentence about what you observe. Use a capital letter to begin each sentence, and end each sentence with the correct punctuation.

Answers will vary.

Answers will vary.

Answers will vary.

Answers will vary.

Read each set of facts. Write one compound sentence that includes both facts. Use a comma and a conjunction word, like and, but, or so.

FACTS
Most frogs are carnivorous. They eat other small animals.
Most frogs are carnivorous, so they eat other animals.

FACTS
Frogs get water through their skin. They do not drink water.
Frogs get water through their skin, so they do not drink water.

FACTS
Some types of frogs live in trees. Others live underground.
Some types of frogs live in trees, but others live underground.

Break this compound sentence. Then write the two facts as separate sentences.
Frogs do not have ears that you can see, but they can hear well.
Frogs do not have ears that you can see. They can hear well.

Write a sentence about what you think each frog will do next.

glass frog — **Answers will vary.**

ghost frog — **Answers will vary.**

flying frog — **Answers will vary.**

leaf frog — **Answers will vary.**

Look at the pictures. Then write a sentence in each thought bubble to show what the frogs are thinking. Last, give the story a title and read it aloud.

TITLE: **Answers will vary.**

Answers will vary.   **Answers will vary.**

Answers will vary.   **Answers will vary.**

Telling a Story

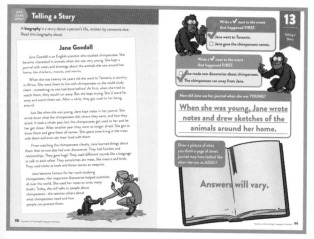

A **biography** is a story about a person's life, written by someone else. Read this biography aloud.

Jane Goodall

Jane Goodall is an English scientist who studied chimpanzees. She became interested in animals when she was very young. She kept a journal with notes and drawings about the animals she saw around her home, like chickens, insects, and worms.

When she was twenty-six years old she went to Tanzania, a country in Africa. She went there to live with chimpanzees so she could study them—something no one had done before! At first, when she tried to watch them, they would run away. But she kept trying. She'd stand far away and watch them eat. After a while, they got used to her being around.

Just like when she was young, Jane kept notes in her journal. She wrote down what the chimpanzees did, where they went, and how they acted. It took a whole year, but the chimpanzees got used to her and let her get closer. About another year they were no longer afraid. She got to know them and gave them all names. She spent some time in the trees with them and even ate their food with them.

From watching the chimpanzees closely, Jane learned things about them that no one else had ever discovered. They had families and relationships. They gave hugs! They used different sounds like a language to talk to each other. They sometimes ate meat, like insects and birds. They used sticks as tools and threw stones as weapons.

Jane became famous for her work studying chimpanzees. Her important discoveries helped scientists all over the world. She used her notes to write many books. Today, she still talks to people about chimpanzees—she teaches others about what chimpanzees need and how people can protect them.

Write a ✓ next to the event that happened FIRST.
☐ Jane went to Tanzania.
☐ Jane gave the chimpanzees names.

Write a ✓ next to the event that happened FIRST.
☑ Jane made new discoveries about chimpanzees.
☐ The chimpanzees ran away from Jane.

How did Jane use her journal when she was YOUNG?
When she was young, Jane wrote notes and drew sketches of the animals around her home.

Draw a picture of what you think a page of Jane's journal may have looked like when she was an ADULT.
Answers will vary.

Jane Goodall kept a journal to record notes from her days with the chimpanzees. Write to record your own events and memories.

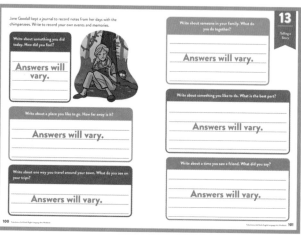

Write about something you did today. How did you feel?
Answers will vary.

Write about a place you like to go. How far away is it?
Answers will vary.

Write about one way you travel around your town. What do you see on your trips?
Answers will vary.

Write about someone in your family. What do you do together?
Answers will vary.

Write about something you like to do. What is the best part?
Answers will vary.

Write about a time you saw a friend. What did you say?
Answers will vary.

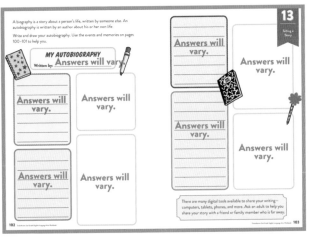

A biography is a story about a person's life, written by someone else. An autobiography is written by an author about his or her own life.

Write and draw your autobiography. Use the events and memories on pages 100–101 to help you.

MY AUTOBIOGRAPHY

Written by: Answers will vary.

Answers will vary.

Answers will vary.

Answers will vary.

Answers will vary.

Answers will vary.

Answers will vary.

Answers will vary.

There are many digital tools available to share your writing—computers, tablets, phones, and more. Ask an adult to help you share your story with a friend or family member who is far away.

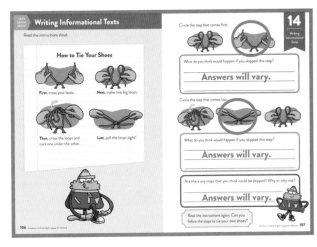

Writing Informational Texts

Read the instructions aloud.

How to Tie Your Shoes

First, cross your laces.

Next, make two big loops.

Then, cross the loops and tuck one under the other.

Last, pull the loops tight!

Circle the step that comes first.

What do you think would happen if you skipped this step?

Answers will vary.

Circle the step that comes last.

What do you think would happen if you skipped this step?

Answers will vary.

Are there any steps that you think could be skipped? Why or why not?

Answers will vary.

Read the instructions again. Can you follow the steps to tie your own shoes?

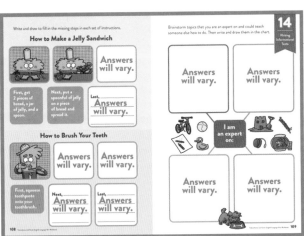

Write and draw to fill in the missing steps in each set of instructions.

How to Make a Jelly Sandwich

First, get 2 pieces of bread, a jar of jelly, and a spoon.

Next, put a spoonful of jelly on a piece of bread and spread it.

Answers will vary.

Last, Answers will vary.

How to Brush Your Teeth

First, squeeze toothpaste onto your toothbrush.

Answers will vary.

Answers will vary.

Next, Answers will vary.

Last, Answers will vary.

Brainstorm topics that you are an expert on and could teach someone else how to do. Then write and draw them in the chart.

Answers will vary.

Answers will vary.

I am an expert on:

Answers will vary.

Answers will vary.

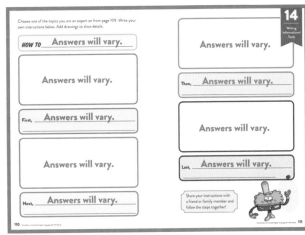

Choose one of the topics you are an expert on from page 109. Write your own instructions below. Add drawings to show details.

HOW TO Answers will vary.

Answers will vary.

First, Answers will vary.

Answers will vary.

Next, Answers will vary.

Then, Answers will vary.

Answers will vary.

Last, Answers will vary.

Share your instructions with a friend or family member and follow the steps together!

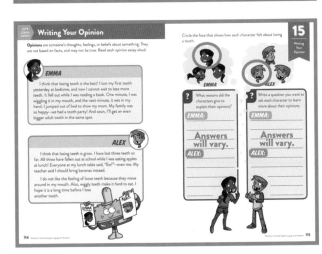

Writing Your Opinion

Opinions are someone's thoughts, feelings, or beliefs about something. They are not based on facts, and may not be true. Read each opinion essay aloud.

EMMA

I think that losing teeth is the best! I lost my first tooth yesterday at bedtime, and now I cannot wait to lose more teeth. It fell out while I was reading a book. One minute, I was wiggling it in my mouth, and the next minute, it was in my hand. I jumped out of bed to show my mom. I was so happy—we had a tooth party! And soon, I'll get an even bigger adult tooth in the same spot.

ALEX

I think that losing teeth is gross. I have lost three teeth so far. All three have fallen out at school while I was eating apples at lunch! Everyone at my lunch table said, "Ew!"—even me. My teacher said I should bring bananas instead.

I do not like the feeling of loose teeth because they move around in my mouth. Also, wiggly teeth make it hard to eat. I hope it is a long time before I lose another tooth.

Circle the face that shows how each character felt about losing a tooth.

EMMA   ALEX

? What reasons did the characters give to explain their opinions?

EMMA:
Answers will vary.
ALEX:

? Write a question you want to ask each character to learn more about their opinions.

EMMA:
Answers will vary.
ALEX:

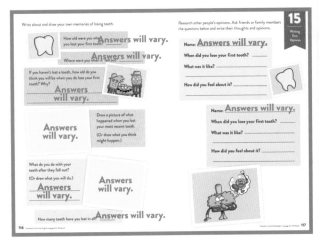

Write about and draw your own memories of losing teeth.

How old were you when you lost your first tooth? Answers will vary.

Where were you when it fell out? Answers will vary.

If you haven't lost a tooth, how old do you think you will be when you do lose your first tooth? Why? Answers will vary.

Answers will vary.

What do you do with your teeth after they fall out? (Or draw what you will do.) Answers will vary.

Draw a picture of what happened when you lost your most recent tooth. (Or draw what you think might happen.)

Answers will vary.

How many teeth have you lost in all? Answers will vary.

Research other people's opinions. Ask friends or family members the questions below and write their thoughts and opinions.

Name: Answers will vary.

When did you lose your first tooth?

What was it like?

How did you feel about it?

Name: Answers will vary.

When did you lose your first tooth?

What was it like?

How did you feel about it?

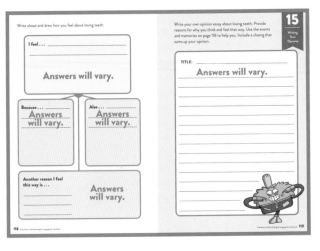

Write about and draw how you feel about losing teeth.

I feel . . .

Answers will vary.

Because . . .
Answers will vary.

Also . . .
Answers will vary.

Another reason I feel this way is . . .
Answers will vary.

Write your own opinion essay about losing teeth. Provide reasons for why you think and feel that way. Use the events and memories on page 118 to help you. Include a closing that sums up your opinion.

TITLE: Answers will vary.

Odd Dot
120 Broadway
New York, NY 10271
OddDot.com

ISBN: 978-1-250-31867-1

WRITER   Megan Hewes Butler

ILLUSTRATOR   Chad Thomas

EDUCATIONAL CONSULTANT   Lindsay Frevert

CHARACTER DESIGNER   Anna-Maria Jung

COVER ILLUSTRATOR   Anna-Maria Jung

BACK COVER ILLUSTRATION   Chad Thomas

BADGE EMBROIDERER   El Patcha

LEAD SERIES DESIGNER   Carolyn Bahar

INTERIOR DESIGNERS   Abby Denning and Colleen AF Venable

COVER DESIGNERS   Carolyn Bahar and Colleen AF Venable

EDITOR   Nathalie Le Du

Our books may be purchased in bulk for promotional, educational, or business use. Please contact your local bookseller or the Macmillan Corporate and Premium Sales Department at (800) 221-7945 ext. 5442 or by email at MacmillanSpecialMarkets@macmillan.com.

DISCLAIMER
The publisher and authors disclaim responsibility for any loss, injury, or damages that may result from a reader engaging in the activities described in this book.

TinkerActive is a trademark of Odd Dot.
Printed in China by Hung Hing Off-set Printing Co. Ltd., Heshan City, Guangdong Province
First edition, 2019

10 9 8 7 6 5 4 3 2 1

For the activity on page 27

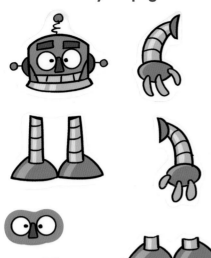

For the activity on page 56–57

For the activity on page 40–41

Sticker your **TINKERACTIVE EXPERT** poster after you complete each project.

_____
(Your Name Here)

IS A TINKERACTIVE EXPERT!

PLACE YOUR MATH BADGE HERE!

PROJECT 1
PROJECT 2
PROJECT 3
PROJECT 4
PROJECT 5
PROJECT 6
PROJECT 7
PROJECT 8
PROJECT 9
PROJECT 10
PROJECT 11
PROJECT 12
PROJECT 13
PROJECT 14
PROJECT 15

PLACE YOUR SCIENCE BADGE HERE!

PROJECT 1
PROJECT 2
PROJECT 3
PROJECT 4
PROJECT 5
PROJECT 6
PROJECT 7
PROJECT 8
PROJECT 9
PROJECT 10
PROJECT 11
PROJECT 12
PROJECT 13
PROJECT 14
PROJECT 15

PLACE YOUR ENGLISH LANGUAGE ARTS BADGE HERE!

PROJECT 1
PROJECT 2
PROJECT 3
PROJECT 4
PROJECT 5
PROJECT 6
PROJECT 7
PROJECT 8
PROJECT 9
PROJECT 10
PROJECT 11
PROJECT 12
PROJECT 13
PROJECT 14
PROJECT 15

 COLLECT THEM ALL!